Business Succession Planning FOR DUMMIES

by Arnie Dahlke

WILEY

John Wiley & Sons, Inc.

Business Succession Planning For Dummies®

Published by
John Wiley & Sons, Inc.
111 River St.
Hoboken, NJ 07030-5774
www.wiley.com

WILEY

About the Author

Arnie Dahlke has a PhD in psychology from the University of Minnesota. Over the years, he has taught full time in both psychology, business, and organizational development departments, served as a director of research for the American Institutes for Research, and worked as an independent consultant.

Arnie has assisted both private (for-profit and nonprofit) and public organizations, using coordinated team-building strategies and process-improvement tools. He brings people together in a spirit of mutual trust, cooperation, and constructive problem solving. As described on his website (www.arniedahlke.com), he helps people in organizations cultivate both continual improvement and customer-responsive mindsets.

Arnie's private-sector clients have included larger corporations, such as Chevrolet, Saturn, Coca-Cola, Gelson's: The Super Market, and Northgate Market; healthcare facilities, such as counseling centers and Northside Hospital; smaller organizations, such as the law firm of Ferruzzo & Ferruzzo, Able Computer, New Media Broadcasting Company, The Party Staff, and Your Staff; and automobile dealerships representing a variety of franchises, including Chevrolet, Chrysler, Ford, Honda, Infiniti, Mitsubishi, Nissan, and Toyota. His work has helped companies win national awards. As a consultant to the Human Interaction Research Institute of Westwood, California, he conducted interviews in California, Missouri, Nevada, Texas, and Utah at local community mental-health centers for the purpose of identifying the factors that go into the sustaining or non-sustaining of innovative procedures in organizational settings.

Arnie's public-sector clients have included both cities and county departments. He has assisted city- and county-management staff, police departments, libraries, and planning and public-works departments in such cities as Washington, D.C., and Los Angeles, Santa Ana, San Bernardino, Santa Rosa, and Torrance, California.

Throughout his career, Arnie has kept alive his love for teaching. He has taught courses and seminars in psychology, organizational behavior, and organizational consulting. He has taught at all levels, from adult students to college freshmen to graduate students at many colleges and universities, including Antioch University, the California School of Professional Psychology, Marymount College, Phillips Graduate Institute, Ryokan College, the University of California, the University of Maryland, the University of Minnesota, the University of Nevada, and the University of Oklahoma.

Dedication

I dedicate this book to all employees, because their morale and futures are dependent on the quality and successful implementation of succession plans in their organization.

Author's Acknowledgments

I appreciate the help of everyone who has helped me put this book together. It has been an exciting, although somewhat exhausting, experience, and it's taught me that you never know how much you know until you start putting it down on paper. I was surprised to find how much I know.

A special thank-you first to my brilliant in-home editor, my wife, Lesli, who pays attention to the slightest detail and improves what I do in subtle but dramatic ways. She has tirelessly supported my efforts through thick and thin, including very long hours spent writing.

I also want to thank Erin Mooney at John Wiley & Sons for giving me the opportunity to write this book; Ken Lloyd for his insightful comments and technical suggestions; and Elizabeth Kuball for her patience, helpful suggestions, and meticulous editing.

Publisher's Acknowledgments

We're proud of this book; please send us your comments at http://dummies.custhelp.com. For other comments, please contact our Customer Care Department within the U.S. at 877-762-2974, outside the U.S. at 317-572-3993, or fax 317-572-4002.

Some of the people who helped bring this book to market include the following:

Acquisitions and Editorial

Project Editor: Elizabeth Kuball

Acquisitions Editor: Erin Calligan Mooney

Copy Editor: Elizabeth Kuball

Assistant Editor: David Lutton

Editorial Program Coordinator: Joe Niesen

Technical Editor: Ken Lloyd, PhD

Senior Editorial Manager: Jennifer Ehrlich

Editorial Manager: Carmen Krikorian

Editorial Assistants: Rachelle S. Amick, Alexa Koschier

Art Coordinator: Alicia B. South

Cover Photos: © iStockphoto.com / james steidl

Cartoons: Rich Tennant (www.the5thwave.com)

Composition Services

Project Coordinator: Katherine Crocker

Layout and Graphics: Joyce Haughey, Corrie Niehaus

Proofreader: Sossity R. Smith

Indexer: Sharon Shock

Publishing and Editorial for Consumer Dummies

   Kathleen Nebenhaus, Vice President and Executive Publisher

   Kristin Ferguson-Wagstaffe, Product Development Director

   Ensley Eikenburg, Associate Publisher, Travel

   Kelly Regan, Editorial Director, Travel

Publishing for Technology Dummies

   Andy Cummings, Vice President and Publisher

Composition Services

   Debbie Stailey, Director of Composition Services

Contents at a Glance

Table of Contents

Introduction

People come and people go in every organization, from large corporations to small family businesses. Some departures are planned and some are unexpected. Your innovative CEO retires. A key programmer in your IT department decides to take a job elsewhere. Your CFO has a heart attack.

When key people leave your organization, you're faced with the task of replacing them. If you have no succession plan in place, a departure can cause waves of disruption to spread throughout your organization. But if you've taken the time to lay out a careful succession plan, the departure may be a mere ripple. It's up to you.

About This Book

I wrote this book to help you develop and implement a fully functioning succession plan. *Business Succession Planning For Dummies* includes a wide range of tips, techniques, and strategies for defining your succession needs, identifying and developing successor candidates, and effectively bringing them onboard.

Every chapter in this book stands on its own. You don't have to read the book from beginning to end. Simply choose the chapter that fits your needs, and dive in!

Conventions Used in This Book

I use the following conventions throughout this book to make the material easy to understand:

- All web addresses appear in `monofont`. When this book was printed, some web addresses may have needed to break across two lines of text. If that happened, rest assured that we haven't put in any extra characters (such as hyphens) to indicate the break. So, when using one of these web addresses, just type in exactly what you see in this book, pretending as though the line break doesn't exist.
- **Bold** is used to highlight the action parts of numbered lists.
- When I introduce a new term, I *italicize* it and define it shortly thereafter, often in parentheses.

Foolish Assumptions

As I wrote this book, I made some assumptions about you, my reader:

- ✔ **You're a manager or human resource professional, and you want to implement a long-term succession plan for your organization.**

- ✔ **You want a smoothly functioning organization today and in the future.** You know problems will occur. You know people will come and go. But you value doing whatever it takes to be prepared.

- ✔ **People are your most important resource.** Yes, you need to make a profit. Yes, your long-term success depends on having a stable customer base. But it's your people who make those things happen.

- ✔ **Key positions exist throughout your organization.** Yes, the loss of your high-powered CEO would be very disruptive. But your organization also would suffer if it lost other key talents: the IT specialist, the brilliant CFO, the star salesperson. . . . People in many key positions make major contributions to your organization's success.

- ✔ **You see the value of having the right person in a key position.** You'd rather have the right person in the right job than place a person in a position and hope that things work out. You believe that having the right person in a key position is critical to your organization's success.

- ✔ **You see the importance of planning.** Yes, planning takes time, and people are busy doing their regular jobs. Nonetheless, you recognize the importance of planning now in order to avoid problems in the future.

- ✔ **You need some help.** You've tried to develop a succession plan. You may even have one halfway finished. Or you may have a finished one that just doesn't seem to be working the way it should. Whatever the case, you need some help.

How This Book Is Organized

Business Succession Planning For Dummies is divided into five parts. Here's what each part covers.

Part 1: What Is a Succession Plan, and Why Do You Need One?

This part is focused on the importance of having a well-developed succession plan. Here I tell you why you need a succession plan in the first place and which type of succession plan you need. I also tell you some of the consequences of *not* having a succession plan and some of the benefits of planning (in case you aren't convinced that succession plans matter).

Part II: Creating a Plan and Putting It into Action

This part is focused on the mechanics of preparing and implementing a succession plan and monitoring and evaluating its success. Here I tell you how to build your succession-planning team, establish the specific goals of your plan, successfully implement your plan, evaluate the plan, and handle obstacles along the way.

Part III: Diving Deeper into Succession Planning

In this part, I show you how to customize your succession plan for various key positions. You find out how to determine the competencies needed for those positions, as well as develop the competencies of potential successors within your organization. Finally, this part shows you how to ensure a smooth transition.

Part IV: Keeping the Succession Ball Rolling

Your work isn't over after you've written your plan. You need to make sure that your plan is well maintained and able to adapt to changes in your organization, its marketplaces, and the economy and society at large. In this part, I tell you what you need to do before, during, and after someone's exit. I explain how to identify changes taking place in the workplace and determine the impact of those changes on your organization. Finally, I guide you through adjusting your succession plan in response.

Part V: The Part of Tens

Every *For Dummies* book ends with a Part of Tens, and this book is no different. In this part, I provide ten common mistakes to avoid and ten ways to keep your plan alive.

Icons Used in This Book

Throughout this book, I use three icons to highlight different kinds of information. Here's what they mean:

You don't have to memorize the information in this book — there is no test at the end — but the Remember icon highlights important information that's especially worth remembering.

The Tip icon points out information that makes the planning process more efficient or just plain easier.

The Warning icon draws your attention to potential pitfalls and danger spots that crop up when implementing a succession plan. Forewarned is forearmed.

Where to Go from Here

If you have no succession plan presently in place, not even a partial one, Part I is a good place to start. If you already have a plan in place, which chapter you'll want to read depends on your needs. For example:

- ✔ If you're having difficulty implementing your existing plan, take a look at Chapter 5 for suggestions on how to make it work and Chapter 7 for tips to overcome implementation obstacles.

- ✔ If you're concerned about the degree of your success in implementing your plan, take a look at Chapter 6 for some tips on monitoring and evaluating your plan.

- ✔ If you need more ideas for identifying and developing successor candidates within your organization, spend some time reading Chapter 10.

When in doubt, the table of contents and index make it easy to find the information you need.

Part I

What Is a Succession Plan, and Why Do You Need One?

The 5th Wave   By Rich Tennant

"Good news, Sir Reginald. The King has elected you his successor to the throne."

In this part . . .

Succession planning will help you clarify the short-term and long-term staffing needs of your organization, and then set up a tailor-made plan to identify, attract, and deploy the right people for the right jobs. It's as much a road map to the future as the future itself!

In this part, you see the many ways in which a succession plan strengthens your organization, ensures the continuity of strong leadership, and establishes a long-range strategy for success. You also discover the basic types of succession plans and how they benefit the needs of your organization, today and in the future.

Chapter 1

Sowing the Seeds for Long-Term Success

· ·

In This Chapter

▶ Clarifying the need for succession planning

▶ Knowing what successful succession plans have in common

▶ Developing and implementing a succession plan

· ·

A succession plan protects your organization's viability as it moves into the future by making sure that qualified talent is available to replace people in key positions who leave the organization.

Ideally, succession planning is an ongoing, continually readjusting process, a process that is woven into your overall strategic plan as a guarantee that your organization won't miss a step when a critical position becomes vacant. Succession planning includes developing replacement talent within the organization, as well as identifying externally available talent sources.

Unfortunately, too many organizations put succession planning on the back burner. A key person leaves, and everyone scrambles to find a replacement. That's short-term thinking. You need to think long-term. In order for your organization to continue to survive and grow in the future, you need to make sure that you're covered if you lose people in critical positions.

You need succession planning.

A few global trends in organizations

The changes taking place in today's world are occurring so rapidly and are so widespread that they're almost impossible to keep up with. Here's a rundown of several key trends that will impact your organization, if they haven't already:

✔ **The globalization of organizations, both for-profit and nonprofit:** Today, more organizations are global than ever before. This means increased interaction among people in different parts of the world with different cultural values and different ways of managing and relating to one another. To thrive in this new world, key people — whether CEOs, upper managers, or other important talent — must have the competencies to deal with such differences. Succession planning is needed to make sure that these competencies aren't lost if and when people leave. For example, if a global corporation with headquarters in the United States is planning a replacement for a corporate leader, potential new hires must be aware of and sensitive to those cultural differences.

✔ **The rapid growth of innovative technologies:** In the past, people shared information and learned through mentoring, face-to-face training, and books and other print media. The explosive sharing of information worldwide has changed much of that. An employee who used to go to her manager to find out how to do something can now get the same information online. Organizations used to recruit talent through newsprint ads, job fairs, networking contacts, and professional associations. Today, increased emphasis is given to recruiting people online. Succession planning is needed to make sure that organizations keep up with these technological advances. Not only do organizations need to train and develop people to be more tech-savvy, but they need a systematic plan to make sure that when people leave, new candidates will be equally tech-savvy.

✔ **The expansion of the multigenerational workplace:** Surveys show that we now have more generations working together in the workplace than ever before. Each generation brings its own set of values, attitudes, behaviors, ways of relating to one another, and ways of working. Effectively managing these different generations is a challenge. Succession planning is needed to make sure that organizations are able to deal with that challenge. For example, when hiring replacements for managers who leave, you need to select people who are capable of dealing with such generational differences.

Why You Need Succession Planning

Today's world of work is changing in ways that are affecting organizations more than ever before in history. More and more employees are changing careers and jumping jobs. New generations — with their different values, behaviors, and expectations — are reshaping the workplace. Increasing cultural diversity is challenging the way managers manage. As a result, the need for continuous succession planning is greater than ever.

What happens when you don't have a succession plan

Not having a succession plan puts the future of your organization at risk. In this highly competitive, fast-paced world, you need every resource you can get. In every position — from your CEO to your IT technician — you need the talent required to keep up with the times.

Not having a succession plan in place when you lose key talent, especially if it happens unexpectedly, can cause all kinds of problems:

- ✔ An often confusing lack of clarity about your organizational direction
- ✔ Anxiety among employees, which leads to a drop in their motivation, satisfaction, and morale
- ✔ Lower quality of service provided to your customers
- ✔ A drop in productivity
- ✔ Delays in completing critical projects
- ✔ A loss of critical knowledge
- ✔ Diminished flexibility in responding to market challenges
- ✔ A decline in the company's reputation, image, and credibility

When these kinds of things happen, your organization may find itself losing out to the competition — organizations that have succession plans in place to cover potential losses of talent.

What a succession plan can do for you

A dynamic, updated succession plan does the following:

- ✔ Conveys to people throughout your organization that you have a clear sense of direction and you're supporting it by properly managing your talent
- ✔ Prevents anxiety among employees stemming from worry about where the organization may be going
- ✔ Ensures that you have the talent to deliver the kind of quality of services you want to deliver

✔ Ensures the kind of talent that will help you maintain high levels of productivity

✔ Helps you avoid any delays that would occur in critical projects due to the departure of needed personnel

✔ Gives you a vehicle for making sure that critical knowledge is passed on to new people

✔ Gives you the flexibility you need to respond to market challenges by maintaining and even improving talent in key positions

✔ Helps you more effectively implement your strategic business plan

✔ Helps you identify potential talent throughout your organization

✔ Helps people in your organization see opportunities for career advancement

✔ Helps you identify any needed training or other kinds of personnel development to maintain the kind of talent you need

✔ Helps maintain your company's reputation, image, and credibility

Taken together, these benefits of an effective succession planning process will help your organization be more competitive and successful in the marketplace.

What Makes a Succession Plan Successful

Different types and sizes of organizations have different succession plans to meet their organizational needs. But all succession plans have some things in common. In this section, I walk you through the key characteristics of every successful succession plan, and then tell you how your succession plan may vary based on your organization's needs.

The key characteristics of a successful succession plan

Every successful succession plan has the following key characteristics:

✔ **It's linked to the organization's overall strategic plan.** The succession plan is guided by your organizational vision and mission.

✔ **It's supported by the organization's upper management.** To get the widespread support that you need for a successful succession plan, the plan must be supported by top management, including your board of directors if you have one.

✔ **It's developed by a succession-planning team.** The succession-planning team should include people from different levels and parts of the organization. Members of the planning team should be familiar with the skills that are needed for the key positions that make up the plan. If the organization is large enough to have an HR department, HR must play a key role in the planning team.

✔ **It's the result of an open planning process.** The planning process needs to be openly communicated throughout the organization, enabling employees at all levels to offer suggestions or voice their concerns.

✔ **It evolves over time.** Your succession plan must not be a static, one-time-only kind of plan. It must literally be an ongoing process — a process that continually monitors your organization's key personnel needs and ensures that available talent will always be available. The plan also should be monitored periodically so that you can evaluate how well the plan is working. The planning team should be ready to make adjustments to the planning process when necessary.

✔ **It includes strategies for developing talent within the organization.** This gives employees opportunities to build stronger commitments to the organization and raises their skill levels, morale, and productivity along the way.

✔ **It searches for talent both within and outside the organization.** The goal is to have the right talent for the right position at the right time.

How succession plans vary in different types of organizations

Even though most successful succession plans share a number of key characteristics (see the preceding section), different kinds of organizations have different needs. In the following sections, I cover some of the more common types of organizations and their particular needs.

Large, for-profit corporations

Such corporations typically have more complex structures that require a more comprehensive succession plan operating at many levels of the organization. For example, if a corporation has gone global, the succession plan has to provide for finding replacement personnel who are cognizant of and comfortable with diverse cultural differences.

Nonprofit organizations

Dependent on fundraising to survive, nonprofit organizations often have difficulty paying executives at a rate that's competitive with for-profit corporations. In addition, founders of nonprofit organizations are often passionate, unique entrepreneurs, and replacing them is a major challenge.

A nonprofit organization can overcome these challenges by fundraising so that it can offer competitive salaries. It also can widen its search for a successor with the right mix of passion and entrepreneurship.

Government organizations

Government executives and other key talent are paid less than their private-sector counterparts, making it difficult to attract the appropriate talent. Plus, the growth of distrust and dislike for the government in recent years has diminished the available supply of talent to fill needed vacancies. To make matters worse, government organizations have trouble developing leadership talent because each agency requires distinct leadership competencies.

The best overall solution for all these problems is to focus on and devote major resources to developing candidates within the organization, in order to prepare them as potential successors.

Colleges and universities

Colleges and universities frequently have more complex bureaucratic procedures, which complicates succession planning. In addition, there are many more constituents to please — such as trustees, administrators, donors, alumni, and students — which makes succession planning a far more complex process.

There are two ways of succeeding in this complicated environment:

- ✔ Make sure that the succession planning team is comprised of people who represent each critical constituency.

- ✔ Set up a rigorous schedule for those team members to obtain approval from their respective constituencies as the plan is being developed.

Partnerships

Frequently, a managing partner persists in hanging on to power long after the time to make a graceful exit has passed. Pride and big egos become stumbling blocks to a smooth transition of leadership.

In addition, the power struggle that often occurs among other key figures in the partnership makes it difficult to develop an effective succession plan.

The best solution to these problems is to engage the services of an expert consultant who can facilitate, coach, and negotiate solutions among the people involved.

Family-owned businesses

Family discord often gets in the way of succession planning when children of the founder/owner can't agree on who gets what and who runs the business. To make matters worse, different family members have different visions of where the organization should be going. IRS regulations that lead to tax liability problems also can complicate succession planning.

The best solution to these problems is to hire a consultant who can facilitate, coach, and negotiate solutions among the people involved.

Responding to different needs

Succession planning also varies according to an organization's specific needs. Have you unexpectedly lost the CEO or other key manager? Given the aging Baby Boomer population, are you anticipating many retirements? Are you focused on making sure that you have the kind of talent you need to carry out your long-range strategic plan?

These different needs can shape the focus of a succession plan in any kind of organization. Here are some of the kinds of plans that can meet an organization's unique needs:

- **Emergency succession plans:** These plans are put into place suddenly, because a key talent has unexpectedly died or left the organization.

- **CEO succession plans:** These plans are designed to ensure that an organization continues to successfully function if it loses its current CEO. This type of plan is particularly popular in family-owned businesses and small partnerships.

- **Transition plans:** Transition plans cover people who have planned an extensive absence for a vacation, the care of a sick relative, a temporary assignment in some other location, and so on.

- **Departure-defined transition plans:** These transition plans are aimed more specifically at positions being vacated due to planned retirements.

- ✓ **Simple replacement plans:** These plans cover any position in an organization.

- ✓ **Talent development plans:** These plans are focused on identifying people who have the potential competencies to be promoted and/or moved into different positions in your organization.

- ✓ **Talent pool plans:** These plans are directed at identifying current sources of needed potential talent in the face of possible departures.

- ✓ **Strategic leadership development plan:** These plans are centered on providing the training and competency development needed by potential leaders in the organization in order to achieve the mission and goals specified in the overall strategic plan.

The best kind of succession plan is actually a process, ongoing and consistently adjusted to keep up with your organization's needs. It focuses more broadly on ensuring that you have the right talent to meet your long-term organizational challenges, such as handling planned product and/or service changes, preparing for anticipating market changes, and so on.

How to Establish Your Succession Plan

Establishing a succession plan is like any other planning you do in your organization: You develop the plan, you implement it, you deal with any implementation obstacles, and you adjust the plan as needed.

Developing the plan

How you develop your plan is, to some degree, a function of the type of organization you have, how broad you want the plan's focus to be, and the specific needs you're addressing. But no matter what the scope of your plan, you'll follow a few standard steps:

1. **Form your team.**

   You want people who are knowledgeable about the positions you're planning to fill and who can help you communicate the plan throughout your organization and gain people's support.

2. **Establish the objectives of your plan.**

   Is your major focus on key leadership positions? Or is it a broader focus that encompasses other key talent in the organization?

3. **Define required competencies.**

   After you've identified the positions to be included in the plan, you need to define the competencies needed for each of those positions.

4. **Identify potential candidate sources.**

   Where will you find the talent you need? Will it come from an external talent source, an internal development talent pool, or both?

5. **Specify implementation steps.**

   You need to know the specific goals you're trying to accomplish with the succession plan, the time by which you want to accomplish each goal, and the people who will be responsible for making sure that each step is carefully pursued and completed.

6. **Specify a monitoring and evaluation strategy.**

   Your plan, especially if you'll be treating it as an ongoing process (which you should!), needs to be monitored and evaluated so that you can adjust it wherever you need to, to make it more successful.

After you've developed your succession plan (hopefully, as an ongoing succession planning process), you're ready to implement it.

Implementing the plan

Implementing a succession plan essentially means converting it into a step-by-step action plan that includes the following:

- ✔ A list of clearly stated objectives for each element of your plan

- ✔ A detailed description of what must be done to achieve each objective

- ✔ A clarification of the inputs needed to achieve each objective, including the specific identification of the people or resources involved

- ✔ A time schedule for accomplishing each objective, which includes how long it should take and when it should be done

✔ The designation of who will be responsible for making sure that each objective is accomplished

✔ A list of potential barriers to successful implementation and suggested actions that could be taken to overcome them if they occur

✔ A set of criteria and metrics for monitoring, evaluating, and adjusting the plan where necessary

 Conceivably, you could start implementing your plan even before it's complete. For example, if, during the planning process, you suddenly have an unexpected departure, you could immediately activate the part of your plan that will address that departure. If you've designed your succession plan as an ongoing adjustable process, you'll find yourself constantly implementing parts of the plan.

Dealing with implementation problems

Like any action plan, problems with implementation are inevitable. Here are some examples:

✔ **As the plan is being implemented, something changes, either in the organization or in the marketplace.** The organization may relocate. A new competitor may emerge with a new approach that requires a different kind of talent. Such changes will lead to revisions in the objectives of one or more elements of the plan.

✔ **The people or resources the plan was depending on may change in the middle of implementation.** If so, you'll need to spend time locating new people or resources.

✔ **In spite of all your careful planning, accomplishing a particular objective may take longer than anticipated.** This may lead to a domino effect, slowing down the accomplishing of other objectives. The succession-planning team may need to adjust its priorities and expectations as a result.

✔ **Economic conditions may unexpectedly worsen, such as during a deep recession.** Your organization may not have the financial resources to pursue particular portions of your succession plan. Your plan will have to be altered to allow you to weather the storm.

✔ **Pressured by your organization's success (or failure), your vision of where you want your organization to go may have to be changed.** Inevitably, this will lead to changes in your succession plan.

> ✔ **Some of the people responsible for implementing elements of your succession plan may not be following through on their responsibilities.** Whatever the difficulties getting in their way, they need to be resolved, or the responsibility for a particular element needs to be reassigned.

Your succession-planning team must be constantly alert to implementation obstacles and available to deal with them. This is why it's so important to make succession planning a *process* rather than simply a *plan.*

Monitoring and evaluating the success of your plan

Make someone on the succession-planning team responsible for continually monitoring and evaluating the plan's implementation, following the evaluation strategy you developed during the planning meetings. More than likely, your evaluation strategy will include collecting data on the following:

✔ The number of vacant positions filled over time as a result of the succession plan

✔ The quality of the performance of those new hires during a specified time frame after hiring

✔ A comparison of how many people have been being hired from within the organization to how many have been recruited from external talent sources

✔ Which talent sources are turning out to be the most fruitful resources in quickly finding replacements

✔ Turnover statistics in the organizational areas addressed by the succession plan

✔ The length of time between notification of an open position and the point at which the position was filled

✔ Employee satisfaction levels, particularly in areas where candidates have been placed through the succession plan

This kind of data can be used to keep the succession-planning team up to date on how successfully the plan's implementation is accomplishing the plan's objectives. It also will identify which elements of the succession plan need to be revised.

The benefits of planning as a process

Change is a constant force. The economy changes. Customer needs change. Your competition changes. Available technologies change. New products and services are constantly being introduced. New generations of workers are reshaping the workplace. All these changes are constantly influencing the functioning of your organization and the degree to which you successfully achieve your mission.

So, you need to establish succession planning as an ongoing process, instead of setting it up only when you it's needed. Anchoring your succession plan to your organization's strategic plan and closely tying it to your HR functions will help you meet the challenges these changes bring. More important, ongoing succession planning can bring several long-range benefits to your organization:

✔ **It provides a greater depth of knowledge about the specific competencies and talents needed in key positions.** Using that knowledge will help you build the kind of workforce needed to make your organization successful.

✔ **It gives your organization more flexibility in finding and maintaining the kind of talent you need.** Your ongoing search for appropriate talent will open doors to new talent sources available to you. The more you build that resource knowledge base, the more flexible you'll be in responding to unanticipated personnel changes.

✔ **Its focus on needed competencies will help you develop potential talent within your organization, which, in turn, will enhance the process of knowledge sharing as an internal candidate takes the place of someone departing.** There's also a very good chance that it will raise the retention levels of your most valuable employees.

✔ **It will more easily yield the people you need to keep up with changes in your strategic plan, changes in the marketplace, changes in the competition, and advances in technology.**

✔ **It will help you build a sense of interdependence among your employees throughout your organization, who will increasingly see themselves as an important part of one organizational team.**

✔ **It will help dispel the typical notion that succession planning is only for CEOs and upper level managers.**

In the long run, all these benefits can help raise the morale of people throughout your organization. In turn, you'll have a more motivated and more productive workforce.

Chapter 2

Why Succession Planning Matters

*I*t's the fourth quarter. There are only 38 seconds left in the game. Your team is behind by five points. It's second down and you're on your opponent's 40-yard line. Winning or losing this game will determine whether you go to the Super Bowl.

Your quarterback drops back to pass. He's immediately overwhelmed and gets sacked by the defense. He crashes to the ground and doesn't get up. During the next few moments, his ardent fans watch in horror as he's carried off the field in a stretcher.

The backup quarterback steps in. He throws a pass to a receiver who's quickly tackled on the 21-yard line. It's now fourth down and, of course, your team decides to go for it. Do or die.

The quarterback fades back, looking for an open receiver, as defense players swarm toward him. Fans watch with bated breath.

And then, it happens. The backup quarterback throws a 40-yard pass to an open receiver who catches it, dodges three tacklers, and sails across the goal line to win the game. The crowd goes wild!

What story could better illustrate the importance of having a succession plan in place in your organization? Whether it's your CEO or some other key talent responsible for your organization's success, you need backup! In this chapter, I explain the many ways that succession planning matters.

Ensuring the Continuation of Competent Leadership

The first reason succession planning matters is that it ensures the continuation of competent leadership, not only the top leadership in your organization but also key leaders at other levels.

Top leadership

Like the captain of a ship, the top leader of your organization is responsible for controlling and maneuvering it as it sails into the future. Along the way, your top leader accumulates a fund of knowledge and acquires valuable experience critical to the success of the organization.

If your top leader unexpectedly departs without your having a designated backup in place, your organization will suddenly become rudderless. The stock of valuable knowledge and experience is lost. Waves of insecurity will spread throughout your organization. Succession planning helps prevent this situation.

 Given the many ways your top leader influences people and processes, there are several compelling reasons why you need to carefully prepare for his or her departure with a succession plan:

- ✔ To ensure that no time or effort is lost as your organization continues to move forward in the pursuit of its objectives

- ✔ To prevent the loss of the fund of knowledge held by your top leader by allowing enough time for him or her to pass it on during a smooth transition to a successor

- ✔ To provide the time needed to help the successor learn from the experience acquired by your departing top leader

- ✔ To maintain a high level of employee confidence in the future of your organization, which, in turn, will help elevate employee morale

- ✔ To preserve high levels of customer confidence in your organization's ability to continue to provide quality products and/ or services throughout the transition process

- ✔ To calm the fears of stockholders and board members about the future of your organization

- ✔ To reassure concerned vendors that your organization will be doing business as usual

- ✔ To prevent any disruptive confusion among employees driven by rumors about the future of your organization

Key leadership at other levels

Your top leader isn't the only person strongly influencing the future of your organization. Division and departmental managers play a significant role in shaping organizational success. Managers are responsible for bringing out the best in their employees. Their management styles and the competencies they bring to their jobs are strong determinants of how well employees perform and, hence, the success of your organization.

In every organization, some highly competent managers stand out more than others. Their presence is critical to the success of the organization. Therefore, it's very important that equally competent successors be available in the event of their departure. Succession planning is the perfect tool for making sure that happens.

Meanwhile, other managers may lack the qualities of highly competent managers but demonstrate both the desire and the potential to improve their own competencies. Comprehensive succession planning includes strategies for helping those managers improve through training, mentoring, and coaching.

And then, there are still other managers who not only lack the competencies required for senior-level positions, but also turn out to be ill suited for their current jobs. Again, succession planning is the perfect tool to deal with this type of situation. With its goal of developing and/or finding high-quality successors for vacant positions, succession planning puts a strong focus on carefully identifying the competencies needed by replacements to insure that there will be trained personnel who are well suited for the vacant positions. When managers are aware of this focus, they're motivated to improve their own competencies. (See Chapter 10 for more on creating a competency culture.)

 By investing time and effort in identifying needed competencies, succession planning will enable you to maintain a continuity of managers with the qualities required to help your organization be successful. It also will focus current managers on their own competencies, stimulating them to improve wherever they can.

Retaining Highly Competent Employees

Leaders and managers are not the only people critical to your organization's success. Ultimately, every employee contributes in some way. The more attention you pay to maintaining a high level of employee competencies, the better your chances of sustaining a successful organization.

Guarding against the loss of key talent

Some people do play more important roles in your organizational success than others, such as the following:

- The talented programmer in your IT department who developed and maintains an outstanding website, which has attracted many new customers to your organization

- The brilliant analyst who has saved your organization significant costs by streamlining forms and procedures in your billing department

- The customer relations supervisor who has skillfully trained and monitored a superb staff that has been highly successful in solving customer problems and maintaining a strong and loyal customer base

- The star of your marketing department who has created and implemented highly successful promotional campaigns

It's particularly essential that key positions such as these be covered without interruption. By applying the steps laid out in your succession plan, you will

- Be able to identify the key positions throughout your organization that are most important to its success

- Gather data by interviewing people currently in those positions and mining other sources (including analyses of competitors) to determine the up-to-date competencies needed by people occupying those key positions

- Provide employees in those key positions with any training needed to make sure their competencies are state-of-the-art

- Identify other people in your organization who have the potential, with some training, to become successor candidates, and provide them with the training they need

- Identify still other people from external sources as potential successors

- As a result, develop a talent pool of possible successors ready and waiting in the wings

Improving competencies throughout your organization

A key component of succession planning is the creation of a *competency profile,* the set of competencies needed for any position in the organization. Competency profiles are important because they

✔ Determine which present and future competencies in each department play a critical role in helping the organization succeed

✔ Yield accurate, up-to-date job information that will provide the basis for job descriptions for every position in your organization

✔ Provide you with the data you need to strengthen your company's performance appraisal and feedback systems

✔ Give employees clear expectations about their jobs, a step that will help them achieve higher performance levels

✔ Establish the competencies needed for employees to reach future job standards, expectations, and objectives

✔ Provide information that will help you create a facilitative work environment for stimulating high performance among all employees

✔ Allow you to spot competency gaps and rectify them by making sure that the right people are in the right jobs

✔ Give you the ability to spot qualified successors for key positions, a step that will result in a continuing supply of competent candidates

✔ Help you redefine and improve your selection criteria when looking at new people

The higher the overall level of competencies in your organization, the better your chances of success.

Providing employee development

Another important component of effective succession planning is clarifying the actions to take in order to develop employees. This succession-planning tool does the following:

✔ Provides the data you need to help employees create individual development plans that will not only help them become more competent at what they do, but also give them opportunities to move to other positions in the organization

✔ Offers employees a mix of internal and external sources of education to help employees develop their competencies

✔ Gives employees the opportunity for training through online courses, in-house programs, special websites, and/or various educational institutions

✔ Helps employees develop their competencies by providing them with targeted coaching and mentoring

✔ Gives employees new work assignments that will help them practice and/or expand their competencies

✔ Offers employees opportunities to rotate to other jobs and explore additional developmental opportunities

TIP

This component of your succession planning matters big time. It will lead to more motivated employees while raising competency levels throughout your organization.

Offering advancement opportunities

A special case of employee development is providing people with opportunities to advance to managerial and leadership positions, if that's what they want. As a vehicle to help people advance themselves, succession planning will

✔ Provide you with a richer understanding of what it takes to be a leader in your organization because of the identification and clarification of required competencies

✔ Make HR staff and managers more aware of the aspirations of individual employees and signal to them that your organization is interested in their well-being

✔ Encourage employees to attend appropriate workshops or seminars, where the information they gather benefits not only them but the rest of your organization

✔ Strengthen the employees' leadership capabilities at every level of your organization

✔ Reduce the chances that you'll move an employee to a key position for the wrong reasons

✔ Let everyone who's even remotely interested in being promoted know far more about the required knowledge, skills, and abilities

Reaping the benefits of a competency-driven culture

Having a succession plan in place that focuses on retaining key talent and improving the competencies of people throughout your organization by providing them with development and advancement opportunities is beneficial to your organization as a whole. Here's how:

- ✔ With an active focus on developing and maintaining high competency levels, your employees will feel more engaged and satisfied, two factors that help keep turnover low.

- ✔ When your organization values talented people at every level, employees will have a greater appreciation of the contributions that everyone makes. This, in turn, facilitates a climate of interdependence, collaboration, and teamwork at all levels.

- ✔ The focus on competency, with all the analyses and data generated as a result, will enable HR to develop recruiting and retention strategies that more effectively align hiring practices to business goals. In the long run, this will significantly contribute to organizational stability and growth.

- ✔ Maintaining high competency levels will raise the overall quality of work produced and services provided to your customers.

- ✔ As a result, your customers will be more satisfied, an outcome that is likely to lead to increased revenues and an expansion of your customer base.

In the long run, the higher the level of competencies in your organization, the better its financial performance will be.

Keeping Up with 21st-Century Trends

A comprehensive succession plan is more than just a simple replacement plan designed to cover vacant positions when people leave. It's a long-range, proactive strategy for building an organization staffed with highly competent people who deliver high-quality products and services. As such, it's a valuable tool, inextricably linked to your strategic plan.

Think about it: Your strategic plan *is* a plan for the future.

Most successful organizations have one foot in the future, always alert to social and economic trends, while anticipating the challenges they bring. The new challenges call for new competencies. That's where succession planning comes in.

Succession planning matters a great deal when you view it as *strategic succession planning.* It lays out the tools and methods for adapting to the trends and challenges of the 21st century.

Globalization

The business world has become global. A significant phenomenon taking place in the globalization of business today is the outsourcing of work to countries in which workers are paid far less than they're paid in the United States. As a result, much of the U.S. economy has shifted from manufacturing to services. In the middle of the 20th century, one-third of employees were employed in manufacturing. Today, that number has dropped to 10 percent, while 80 percent of people are working in service organizations.

More organizations are enmeshed in international business ecosystems, interacting with vendors and suppliers in other countries. As a result, top leaders and managers need to be more aware of, and sensitive to, cultural differences.

More and more businesses are turning into global corporations and establishing or contracting with facilities in other countries. As a consequence, managing the culturally diverse workforce has become a major challenge.

Adapting to these challenges means thinking strategically as you implement the steps of your succession-planning process:

- As positions open up or as new positions are created by changes in the marketplace, your succession plan gives you the tools and methods you need to redefine the competencies needed by people engaged in our service-oriented economy.

- Similarly, given the cross-cultural challenge of dealing with companies in other countries, your succession plan gives you tools and methods for redefining the competencies needed by candidates to fill vacant or new positions that deal with your overseas vendors and suppliers.

- Different leadership and management styles are needed to deal with different cultural groups. It's particularly important that your CEO and key managers acquire and exercise the leadership and management competencies needed to deal with a more culturally diverse workforce. Strategic succession planning will help you do that.

The Internet information explosion

Advances in Internet technology have led to sharing of information among people in diverse settings.

You no longer need to have a newspaper delivered to your front door. Go online. Not only will you find the same information that appears in your delivered newspaper, but it will be more up to the minute.

You no longer need to go to a bookstore to buy a book. Now you can simply order books online from a variety of sites. Even easier, download an ebook to your iPad, Kindle, or Nook.

You no longer need to go to a library to search through card-catalog drawers. You simply go online to the library website and search for whatever book you want.

Researchers developing new products used to have to page through shelves of journals to get the information they needed. Now, by registering at specific websites, they can download practically any journal they need.

Sites such as SlideShare (`www.slideshare.net`) allow you to upload and share presentations with colleagues, no matter where they are. Sites such as GoToMeeting (`www.gotomeeting.com`) and WebEx (`www.webex.com`) enable you to hold meetings, seminars, and videoconferences with people worldwide.

Cloud computing, an Internet technology that uses remote servers to maintain data and software, enables organizations to use software without installation, giving them the ability to access personal files at any computer with Internet access.

Mobile computing and phone apps are increasingly used in devices such as laptops, smartphones, and tablets.

This Internet information explosion is changing the way work is being done:

- ✔ With easy and efficient Internet access, many companies are allowing people to work from home, at least part-time.

- ✔ Using Internet information technology gets things done faster, more efficiently, and at lower costs.

- ✔ The speed with which employees can access information online enables them to more effectively multitask.

- ✔ The multitude of information sources and ideas online provide great stimuli for entrepreneurs.

- ✔ Team members are holding virtual meetings on the Internet. In some cases, team members are working from home and/or are located throughout the world.

- ✔ Seminars are being conducted online to help develop employee competencies, introduce new products, or simply share information needed by various sections of an organization.

✔ Employees are gaining new knowledge and new skills by signing on to instructional websites.

The overall result of these changes is more efficiency, higher productivity, and greater responsiveness to customer needs.

"So," you ask, "what does all this have to do with succession planning?" It's all a matter of competencies. The numerous, constantly evolving Internet options for sharing information call for new sets of skills in the workplace. Your succession plan can help you meet these needs.

Social media

With seemingly no end in sight, the last two decades have spawned new types of social media that have great implications for how people communicate and work with one another. For example:

✔ Social networks, such as Facebook (www.facebook.com), Twitter (www.twitter.com), and LinkedIn (www.linkedin.com) allow users to send messages, share content, and connect with friends and co-workers.

✔ Blogs, hosted on platforms such as Blogger (www.blogger.com), WordPress (www.wordpress.com), and TypePad (www.typepad.com), are essentially online journals where anyone can write about anything he or she wants and share content picked up from other social media sites.

✔ Media-sharing sites, such as Flickr (www.flickr.com) and YouTube (www.youtube.com), enable users to share photos and videos.

✔ Social-bookmarking sites, such as AddThis (www.addthis.com) and Digg (www.digg.com), let people use the Internet to organize, store, manage, and search resources online by saving bookmarks to a public website and "tagging" them with keywords. They also allow users to share pages they find with one another.

✔ Wikis, such as Wikipedia (www.wikipedia.org) and WikiAnswers (http://wiki.answers.com), are sites on which many different users can contribute content any time they want from any place.

✔ Sites such as Yammer (www.yammer.com) and Chatter.com (www.chatter.com) are internal social-media networks that are accessible exclusively to employees of a given company to securely share ideas, news, and updates in real time.

These forms of social media and many more are being increasingly used by people every day. According to the 2011 Nielsen Social Media Report:

- ✔ Twenty-five percent of the time that Americans spend on the Internet is devoted to social networks and blogs.

- ✔ Eighty percent of active Internet users visit social networks.

- ✔ Seventy percent of adults actively using social networks shop online.

- ✔ Fifty-three percent of adults actively using social networks follow a brand.

- ✔ In ten major global markets, social networks and blogs reach over 75 percent of active Internet users.

Like the Internet information explosion, and very much part of it, social media are influencing the way business is being done and work is being performed. Here are some of the ways you can use social media in your organization:

- ✔ To generate new business and increase productivity by allowing employees to work collaboratively online no matter where they are in the world.

- ✔ To advertise your product or service.

- ✔ To discover the needs and wants of customers.

- ✔ To provide customer feedback.

- ✔ To strengthen existing business relationships and market new products or services to existing customers.

- ✔ To stimulate internal communication among employees and encourage them to participate in internal organizational initiatives.

- ✔ To communicate to people throughout the organization about the current status of their organization, new additions in staff and facilities, and plans for the future. As such, it's a perfect tool to help bring people together as one organizational team.

The goal of your succession plan is to fill potential or open positions with people who have the competencies needed for now and the future, and skill with social media is a competency you'll likely need.

The increasing use of social media calls for fresh delineations of competencies. Newly hired employees will need to possess a broad range of proven social media skills. Social-media skills are becoming a critical element of effective succession planning.

On the flip side of the coin, when it comes to recruiting people for vacant or newly established positions, social media can be a very powerful and effective resource. Your succession plan can use social media to recruit the kinds of employees you need to fill required positions. Sources such as Facebook, Twitter, and LinkedIn are wonderful sources of talent and can be used to build your organizational presence as well. In addition, the succession-planning team can use social media to attract talent through such sites as YouTube or company video contests sponsored on your organization's website.

Workforce changes

Today's workforce is made up of a greater mix of generations than any workforce in history. From Traditionalists (born before 1947) to Baby Boomers (born 1947–1965) to Gen Xers (born 1966–1977) to Millennials (born 1977–2000), today's workforce is diverse.

This mixture of the four generations in today's workplace has many implications for the kinds of competencies you identify in your succession planning, because each generation brings with it a unique set of values, expectations, attitudes, preferences, and work styles. Here are just a few examples:

- Traditionalists and Baby Boomers typically prefer conventional mail and face-to-face conversations with people by phone, while Gen Xers and Millennials are more inclined to communicate through the Internet and social media.

- Traditionalists and Baby Boomers plan their work and take it step by step, while Gen Xers and Millennials are more inclined to jump right in and get things moving.

- Traditionalists and Baby Boomers are comfortable with following a hierarchy, while Gen Xers and Millennials tend to be self-starters and more comfortable with a flat organizational structure.

- Traditionalists and Baby Boomers tend to feel that constant performance feedback is a negative thing because they feel scrutinized and judged, while Gen Xers and Millennials appreciate and even need frequent feedback about their performance.

- Millennials are much more interested in innovation and doing things in new ways than earlier generations.

Most important from the standpoint of multigenerational issues and succession planning, millions of Baby Boomers are approaching retirement age — the oldest of the boomers turned 65 on January 1, 2011. Although statistics indicate that many Baby Boomers are planning to work into their 70s, the reality is that employers will soon be facing a tremendous increase in the number of retirements and, therefore, open positions. The mass retirements of Baby Boomers will lead to a serious loss of skilled, experienced, knowledgeable employees, a situation that's compounded by a smaller pool of individuals to take their place across all industries and job levels. In order to lessen the impact of this major shift in the workforce, it's even more critical to identify, train, and develop employees to fill these impending vacancies.

In addition, globalization has brought us a more culturally diverse workforce. As a result, it's important for the succession-planning team to recognize the diversity of the labor force and take careful note of the skill levels of people from different parts of the world, while also paying extra attention to their customs, values, expectations, attitudes, preferences, and work styles.

Given the emerging multigenerational, culturally diverse workplace, new sets of competencies are needed by people at every level from the CEO to front-line employees.

When recruiting successors for any position, job descriptions and required competencies need updating to take into account the new diverse workforce:

- ✔ Management positions call for more flexible management styles, with the ability to adapt to different generations and cultures.

- ✔ Employees at all job levels and in all departments, especially sales, marketing, and customer relations, need to be more competent in the use of social media.

- ✔ Overall, people in any position need to be more techno-savvy.

When identifying and developing potential successors within your organization, coaching and training sessions need to be updated to ensure that candidates possess the right competencies.

If you think of succession planning as *strategic succession planning* as you deal with this modern workforce, you'll recognize the value of conducting periodic training sessions on such topics as communication, team building, diversity, and new technologies for everyone in the organization.

Recognizing the Consequences of Not Having a Succession Plan

Not having an effective succession plan can be detrimental to your organization in many ways:

✔ **You'll lose talented leadership.** In most organizations, leaders play a make-or-break role. When you have an organization that is successful, has been growing, and is likely to continue its success, one of the worst things that can happen is bringing on a new leader who isn't up to the task. Succession planning can help you avoid that kind of catastrophe.

✔ **As a result of losing a talented leader, you'll lose his or her valuable knowledge, skills, and expertise.** A succession plan will facilitate the process of transferring that vast knowledge base to a successor.

✔ **Without a succession plan contributing to the strength, growth, and success of your company, you may damage your local economy because of your company's potential backsliding and corresponding loss of jobs.**

✔ **Without a very visible, ongoing succession plan, employees are more likely to leave because they don't see opportunities for developing themselves or advancing to higher positions.**

✔ **At a minimum, productivity will suffer as employees become less confident in the future of their organization.** Without competent employees and the resulting deterioration of productivity, customer satisfaction and loyalty will decline.

✔ **Your organization could face devastating market consequences, from sinking stock prices (if you're a public corporation) to serious damage to its reputation, goodwill, and overall image in the community and the marketplace.** Studies have shown that more than one-quarter of businesses suffer financially because of poor succession planning.

Chapter 3

Pinpointing the Right Type of Plan for Your Organization

. . . .

In This Chapter

▶ Planning for unexpected departures

▶ Preparing for predictable transitions

▶ Putting together a strategic plan for your organization

. . . .

*S*uccession plans are known by different names in different types of organizations. A for-profit corporation may use different terminology than an academic organization, an academic organization may use different terminology than a government organization, and so on. But regardless of the type of organization, each succession plan falls into one of three categories:

✔ **Plans that deal with unexpected departures:** This type of plan prepares your organization for a quick response to unexpected personnel changes — a sudden death or incapacitating illness, the departure of a key person who decides to take a job elsewhere, and so on.

✔ **Plans that ensure smooth and orderly, predictable transitions:** This type of plan ensures that you'll have replacements for key personnel who are planning a scheduled departure — someone retiring; a planned and extensive absence for a vacation, a sabbatical, or care of a sick relative; a temporary assignment in some other location; and so on.

✔ **Longer-range, strategic succession plans:** This type of plan focuses more broadly on ensuring that you have the right talent to meet your long-term organizational needs — handling planned product and/or service changes, preparing for anticipating market changes, and so on.

A rose is a rose is a rose . . .

All different types of organizations develop succession plans: for-profit organizations, nonprofit organizations, government organizations, volunteer organizations, academic organizations, professional associations, and so on. People in these various types of organizations tend to use their own terminology to refer to succession plans.

Here are some labels you may have heard bandied about in your own organization:

✔ Role-based succession planning

✔ Individual-based succession planning

✔ Internal talent pool succession planning

✔ External talent pool succession planning

✔ Emergency succession planning

✔ Transition succession planning

✔ Replacement succession planning

✔ Workforce planning

✔ Strategic leadership development

✔ Departure-defined succession planning

✔ Family succession planning

Remember: Regardless of what people call a succession plan, the plan falls into one of the three categories described in this chapter.

In this chapter, I introduce you to these three types of plans, so you can determine which type of plan your organization needs first.

Any organization will be best served by developing each of these three types of plans.

Expecting the Unexpected

Every organization, regardless of its size, has key people. A visionary executive whose operational and financial skills have grown a small business into a large, profitable company. A key salesperson who has outperformed not only salespeople within your company but also salespeople in competing companies. An IT genius who has moved your business into the technological 21st century.

An organization can lose key people like these any time, and the loss can be devastating. In fact, the more critical the person, the lower the chance that the organization will recover.

People leave unexpectedly for a number of reasons. They become unexpectedly ill or die. They get offers from other companies. Their spouses or partners take jobs across the country.

 Your organization won't always know in advance when a key person is going to leave, and even if you're given notice, that notice may only be a couple weeks. You need a quick-response plan in place so you don't have to scramble at the last minute to cope with the loss. Here are several steps you can take to make sure that you're prepared for unexpected departures down the road:

1. **Form a specific quick-response team that will be available to address any unexpected departures.**

   Team members need to be capable of fast action and willing and able to spend the time it takes to deal with any unexpected departure. Their primary task is to make sure that operations and services in your organization continue without interruption.

2. **Have the team enlist the help of HR.**

   HR should help the quick-response team do the following:

   - Determine key people. The performance of everyone in your organization is important to its success. However, the loss of some people, such as a visionary leader or a highly talented salesperson, may be more disruptive to the functioning of your organization than the loss of others.

   - Describe the particular talents and competencies that make each person so important to the success of your organization.

   - Based on specific measures of performance and results attained by each person, develop a thorough job description that covers all his or her responsibilities and the priorities associated with each.

   - Develop a list of replacement sources, including people within the organization who have the potential to move into the vacated position, as well as external sources (such as executive websites, search firms, or employment agencies).

3. **Set up a system for periodically reviewing and updating the job descriptions and replacement sources you came up with in Step 2.**

The changing demands of your customers in response to marketplace changes, new competitors, innovations, and so on may call for new or at least revised competencies for particular key people. You need to make sure that this information is always current.

4. **Identify one or two potential backups for each of your key positions, people who, with little preparation, could fill the departing person's shoes until a permanent replacement can be found.**

   If there is a vast gap between your company's key personnel and the rest of their staff, you need to use external sources to put this important step in place.

5. **Make sure the backup people receive any needed coaching, mentoring, or training to get them up to speed.**

Having a quick-response plan in place will minimize any disruption caused by unexpected departures.

What to do if someone leaves before you have a plan in place

If you've just been notified that a key individual has left your company, and you don't already have a succession plan in place, you need to act fast.

Immediately form an emergency transition team. Team members need to be people who are knowledgeable (or very quickly can be brought up to speed) about the competencies of the departing talent. They need to be people who are capable of fast action and are willing and able to spend the time it takes to cover the emergency.

The emergency transition team must initiate several actions:

1. **Determine the impact of the unexpected departure on the way your organization functions.**

2. **Immediately develop a communication strategy that reassures people in the organization who are affected by the departure that steps are being taken to keep things running smoothly.**

   In the case of the CEO or other key manager, the communication strategy will need to reassure people throughout the entire organization.

3. **Identify steps you can take to minimize any damage, including designating people who can temporarily cover the departing person's responsibilities.**

4. **With the help of HR, update the job description and clearly define and describe the talents and competencies needed by any prospective replacement candidate.**

5. Based on the description you created in Step 4, enlist the help of your HR staff to initiate a talent search for potential replacements from within your organization and from external talent sources.

6. Interview prospective candidates as soon as possible.

7. Select and hire the replacement, familiarize the new hire with the organization, and walk him or her through the areas and people most affected by the departure.

Throughout this experience, team members should record and catalog the steps they're taking, any problems they encounter, and the actions they're taking to deal with the problems. All this information will be valuable input to the broader task of preparing for future unexpected departures.

Remember: All along, keep people who are affected by the departure informed of the team's progress.

Laying the Groundwork for Planned Transitions

Dealing with a planned departure — such as someone retiring, going on sabbatical, or being temporarily relocated — is a lot easier than coping with one that happens unexpectedly. Instead of scrambling to cover the loss, you have time to develop an effective transition plan.

How you deal with the transition depends on the person who's leaving and his or her role within the organization.

CEOs or other key leaders

Replacing a CEO or other key leader who has been primarily responsible for the success of an organization is usually a great challenge. The pending departure of this kind of key player can cause anxiety for all kinds of people in your organization:

✔ **The person who's leaving:** Leaving an organization often is very difficult for key executives. Most of them recognize what they've done for the organization and are fearful that no one else can do as well. Some are so used to the exciting jolts of adrenalin they get from their jobs that they don't want to give them up.

✔ **The board of directors:** Board members often feel very nervous about the impact of an executive's departure on the future of the organization. They may pressure the person who's leaving to postpone his or her planned departure.

✔ **People throughout the organization:** Frequently, a key executive is seen as the hero by people throughout the organization. After all, that person was responsible for turning the organization into a success. The pending departure may send ripples of anxiety throughout the organization, possibly resulting in lower morale, as people start worrying about their own futures. Some people even may begin thinking about leaving the organization for a similar position elsewhere.

So, how do you deal with the key executive's planned departure and minimize the anxiety for everyone involved? Here are some suggestions:

✔ Make sure you have an up-to-date list of the key executive's functions. This list should be detailed enough to serve as a kind of helpful road map for the person's replacement.

✔ Establish a leadership transition team made up of people who have interacted with the executive and are very familiar with the organization's strategic plan.

✔ Give the leadership transition team the authority to do whatever they need to do in order to make the transition as smooth as possible.

✔ If you have a board of directors, engage them in the process. Board members typically are aware of and involved in shaping the long-term goals of the organization. They can be very useful in selecting an appropriate replacement candidate.

✔ Carefully review any possible internal candidates for the position. If you find that no current employees have the knowledge, skills, and abilities required for this key leadership role, initiate a search through external sources and resources.

✔ If possible, after a replacement candidate has been identified, have that person shadow the departing executive, including sitting in on manager meetings and other important tasks. The more familiar and comfortable the replacement is with the departing executive's job, the smoother the transition will be.

Keep people throughout the organization informed of what's happening, in order to avoid the spreading of rumors.

Family business owners or organization founders

Another special case of a key person planning a departure is a family business owner who has been primarily responsible for the founding of an organization. This case presents several additional challenges:

✔ Typically, the founder has been involved day after day for so long, and has put so much energy into the business, that the business defines the founder's identity as a person. When the founder leaves the business, his or her identity changes, and that can be a very frightening and difficult life transition. The same applies to the founder's spouse, if he or she played an important role in the business over the years. A potential consequence is a delay in the founder's departure.

✔ In a family business, the founder's children often are involved in the day-to-day operations, or at least expect that one of them will take over the business when the founder leaves. The founder wants to be fair to the children during the succession process, but one son or daughter may be more qualified than the others. This can result in a very painful internal conflict for the founder, causing a delay in departure.

✔ Over the years, managers or other key people in the business likely have developed a close relationship with the founder. The significant change in that relationship upon the founder's departure can cause a great degree of worry and uncertainty about the future, which, in turn, can affect their performance.

✔ The same people, having been in a comfortable, personal relationship with the founder for years, may worry about having to adjust to someone new. They may fear that newly instituted processes or controls will restrict them in the performance of their jobs.

✔ Clients and/or suppliers who have developed a dependent relationship with the founder over the years may become quite concerned how the departure will affect their futures. The founder, after all, is the person they're used to going to when they have a problem or need some action to be taken.

So, how do you deal with such challenges? Here are some suggestions:

✔ Engage the services of an outside consultant or put together an outside advisory group to consult with the founder and help manage his or her departure. The right kind of expertise can minimize the pain associated with the departure.

✔ With the consulting help, the founder should develop a long-range vision of the future when he or she is no longer running the business.

✔ Involve the managers and other key personnel in the business in the development of the long-range vision. Their participation will give them a sense of ownership in the succession process and lessen their fears and misgivings about the founder's departure.

- ✓ Clearly describe the competencies needed to run the business and use that description in discussions with potential successors, whether they're family members or people outside the business.

- ✓ Make it clear to family members that the description will serve as a guideline for selecting the appropriate successor. The more objectively the founder can document what will be required of a successor, the easier it will be for him or her to discuss the topic with family members.

- ✓ Select a successor well in advance of the founder's departure in order to give that person time to be coached and mentored by the founder so that he or she becomes completely familiar with the founder's job and develops comfortable relationships with other people in the business.

- ✓ Develop an estate plan that clearly describes how family assets and any ownership will be distributed among the founder's heirs.

Dealing with your own planned departure

You get an exciting charge out of what you do. You're worried that no one can do it as well. What will happen to your organization if you leave?

Driven by this thinking, your nervous hesitation to leave according to your planned departure may cause a problem for your organization. It may make it difficult for you to be objective enough to spur the development of a succession plan that leads to a smooth transition.

The key is to take actions that will reduce the stress your looming departure is generating. Here are some steps that you can take to put yourself in a comfortable departure frame of mind:

- ✓ Chances are, you take pride in having founded and grown a successful business. Look at your departure as an opportunity to define your legacy by developing an organizational plan for the future that sets it on a path for further growth and success.

- ✓ Make the rounds. Spend time with people in your organization. Show them your appreciation for the work they've done and help them see the potential that you envision for the future.

- ✓ After you've chosen your successor, spend time coaching and mentoring that person, and provide the added assurance that you'll be available for assistance in the future.

- ✓ Do some simple things like organizing your office to make sure that your successor can easily locate key documents.

> ✔ Develop a list of contacts for your successor — names and telephone numbers of people who can be contacted for advice and/or information in various problem areas. Whether in person or by e-mail, introduce your successor to each of these contacts.
>
> ✔ Above all, as you engage in these activities, allow yourself enough time before your departure to gradually and comfortably transfer your duties to your successor. When you depart, this will help you feel confident that your business will continue to thrive and your legacy will be preserved.
>
> If, after taking these actions, you're still feeling stressed and having difficulty parting ways with your organization, hire a coach or consultant to help you move smoothly through the process.

Board members

One of the most important functions of a board of directors is to advise an organization's management. In for-profit, publicly traded organizations, the board has a fiduciary responsibility to protect shareholder assets and ensure a good return on investments. In a community-oriented nonprofit organization, board members generally provide the organization with community contacts and fundraising opportunities. In either case, the board of directors plays an important role in the functioning of the organization.

Here are a few suggestions for dealing with the planned departure of a board member:

- ✔ **Start with a focus on the future.** Your board of directors plays an important role in shaping the future of your organization. So, it's very important that everyone on the board has a clear picture of what you want your organization to achieve in the future.

- ✔ **Look for replacement candidates who have the expertise to meet and even surpass the long-term goals and who can work effectively as part of a team (because that's what a board is).** Make sure the replacement candidate is familiar with and demonstrates a commitment to your organizational mission.

- ✔ **Assess your existing board.** Do you have a good balance of people helpful to your future plans? Is the size of your board suitable for your needs? Do you have the right mixture of people who share the ability to work as a team and have the innovative flexibility to reshape your future plans toward even more success? Answers to these questions will directly influence what kind of replacement(s) you need.

✔ **Search for, interview, and select a new board member or members.** Allow enough time before the planned departure to have the selected new board member sit in on at least a few board meetings to develop a level of interactive comfort among board members.

Special considerations for nonprofit organizations

If you're engaged in succession planning in a nonprofit organization, you're faced with some special considerations:

✔ A large nonprofit organization will have less difficulty absorbing the costs involved in succession planning. But a small nonprofit organization may be challenged by the costs, such as working with executive search firms, advertising, relocating the new hire, and paying the new hire more money. In addition, you may see a drop in revenue because of the loss of donors who had personal relationships with the person who's departing.

✔ A limited number of candidates interested in filling a vacant position because they know they're able to earn better salaries in other organizations.

✔ A limited availability of candidates who have the needed competencies to accomplish the nonprofit's unique mission.

If you're involved with succession planning in the nonprofit organization, particularly if it's a small nonprofit organization, here are a few tips:

✔ As with other types of organizations, succession planning for nonprofit organizations works best if it's an ongoing organizational process. Too many nonprofit organizations with limited funds don't take the time to establish an ongoing succession planning process. In the long term, succession planning is a worthwhile investment of time and resources.

✔ Look within the organization for possible candidates who may be able to assume the duties of the departing person with minimal training and mentoring.

✔ If you have a board of directors, make sure they fully support your succession planning. Enlist their help by getting them to use their connections to find replacement candidates.

✔ Look outside the organization to its volunteers. People volunteer because they're committed to your mission. Somewhere in that group of committed people is a potential replacement.

Remember: As with any succession plan, make sure you keep everyone informed to avoid the negative consequences of anxious people not knowing what's going on.

Special considerations for government organizations

If you're engaged in succession planning in a government organization, you face another set of challenges:

- Government employees, particularly top government executives, are paid less than their private-sector counterparts. This has the effect of both reducing the size of the available talent pool and diluting its quality in terms of the competencies needed.

- In recent years, the size of the available talent pool has shrunk even further due to a growing distrust of and subsequent lowering of interest in government careers. This pool of potential candidates is also decreased as a result of initiatives that focus on reducing the size of government and, consequently, the number of jobs and opportunities in the public sector.

- Complex government bureaucracy limits the flexibility of succession planning. The regulations for hiring and firing people in government organizations are far more complicated than in organizations in the public sector.

- Regulations for promotion and the length of time for being in the position before being promoted further effect smooth succession planning.

- The goals and plans of government organizations frequently change when new administrations come into power, bringing with them changing politics and priorities.

So, what can be done in the face of these challenges? One of the most effective things a government organization can do is to make succession planning an ongoing process, focused on creating a pool of future replacements, instead of focusing on finding replacements when departures occur. This pool can be developed by spotting potential replacement candidates within the organization who, with some training, coaching, and/or mentoring, could quickly assumed the duties of someone departing.

As part of this effort, potential candidates can be assigned special projects that would help them sharpen the competencies they'll need when moved to a new position. In developing such a replacement pool, there should be a high degree of communication with individuals in senior levels of government. This step increases the likelihood of a buy-in from these individuals and, hopefully, increased access to needed resources.

Remember: Effectively communicate these activities throughout the organization, making people aware of opportunities for them to participate.

Taking these steps can have the side benefits of increasing productivity and raising the morale of people who may be considering other opportunities.

There's no question about it: If you have a board of directors, you know how important they are to the organization and how worthwhile it is to spend the time and effort searching for and selecting a member replacement. Don't cheat yourself by trying to accomplish this task too fast.

Strategically Mapping Your Organization's Future

The third type of succession plan is all about strategy — it's about ensuring that your organization has the right talent to meet your long-term organizational needs. In order to know what your long-term organizational needs are, you need a strategic plan (see the nearby sidebar, "Strategic planning: A road map for the future").

An ongoing succession planning process should be part of your strategic plan. Here's why:

- ✔ When a key person, particularly a key leader, plans a departure, your strategic plan will guide you in determining the kind of competencies you'll look for in a replacement candidate.

- ✔ The future evolution of your organization as laid out in your strategic plan will tell you what kind of new and/or different talent you may need to cover any future departures.

- ✔ Changing market conditions, new customer demands, and new competition may lead you to make significant changes in your strategic plan. Such shifts in your long-range thinking will influence your decisions on the competencies and talents needed when replacing departing personnel.

Meeting your current strategic needs

Your strategic plan tells you what kind of talent you currently need. The linking of your ongoing succession planning to your strategic plan enables you to be constantly in touch with what has to be done when someone departs. It enables you to determine several things:

- ✔ The specifications of those positions that are critical to achieving your mission

- ✔ The competencies needed by people who occupy the critical positions

- ✔ High performers in your organization who can potentially fill key vacant positions

> ✔ The kinds of training, coaching, and/or mentoring those high performers will need to become replacement candidates
>
> ✔ Gaps between people you need and people you have available
>
> ✔ Whether particular external sources of talent can supply the number and caliber of personnel that you need

Having this knowledge will make it very easy for you to find suitable replacements for people who depart, whether they're emergency or planned departures.

Planning for your future strategic needs

Your strategic plan tells you what talents and competencies will be needed in the future. The linking of your ongoing succession planning to your strategic plan will point to questions that you have to answer in order to prepare your organization for the future:

> ✔ Do you need to alter your strategies for selecting and developing people in your organization?
>
> ✔ Do you need to provide special training for potential internal candidates to enable them to adapt to future needs?
>
> ✔ Do you need to redesign your recruitment and retention strategies?
>
> ✔ Do you need to identify new pools of prospective candidates for new positions?
>
> ✔ Do you need to restructure your planned job assignment and rotation procedures?

The answers to these questions will guide you to the actions that need to be taken to ensure that your organization is prepared to continue achieving its mission in the future.

Changing your strategic plan

From time to time, events force you to reevaluate and change your long-term strategic plan and redefine your mission statement. As a result, you may find yourself having to radically change the direction of your organization, with the subsequent consequence of having to redefine the characteristics of the kinds of people you need.

Strategic planning: A road map for the future

From its Ancient Greek military roots to the present day, strategic planning has focused on the long-range outcomes of an organization. Your strategic plan is a road map for determining how your organization will survive, thrive, and compete in the marketplace. It determines the kinds of talent you need in your organization to ensure its success. Therefore, your strategic plan is a critical backdrop to any succession planning you may undertake.

If you have a carefully detailed strategic plan, a key departure is an opportunity to reassess your needs and update the plan. If you don't have an updated, carefully detailed strategic plan, now is the time to develop one.

For more on strategic planning, check out *Strategic Planning For Dummies,* by Erica Olsen (Wiley).

Here's where the importance of an ongoing succession planning process becomes very evident. Instead of having to put together a special team to handle the change, the ongoing succession planning process gives you the flexibility to quickly

- ✔ Realign job requirements to accomplish the mission put forth in the revised strategic plan

- ✔ Assess where competency gaps exist between the existing workforce and what you need to achieve the revised strategic plan

- ✔ Design strategies for quickly closing those competency gaps, such as sending potential internal candidates to special training sessions and locating more appropriate external talent pools

- ✔ Broaden your recruitment activities in your search for potential candidates to cover key personnel departures

- ✔ Restructure how you deploy your existing workforce to maximize the probability of successfully achieving your revised mission

- ✔ Determine any external support you may need, such as specialized consultants

People throughout the organization are affected by any changes in the direction of the organization. Revising your strategic plan gives you an opportunity to involve more people in your organization in the succession-planning process, which, in turn, gives them a greater sense of ownership of the changes taking place. They'll feel more secure and connected to your organization as a result.

Part II

Creating a Plan and Putting It into Action

The 5th Wave   By Rich Tennant

"I think Dick Foster should head up that new project. He's got the vision, the drive, and let's face it, that big white hat doesn't hurt either."

In this part . . .

Because preparation is an essential building block for success, this part focuses on the central role that solid preparation plays in the development of a truly effective succession plan. This part answers all the key foundational questions: What is the objective of the plan? What kind of a plan should it be? Who is part of the planning process? How do you link the succession plan to other plans and programs in your organization? After you have your succession plan, how do you implement it?

The answers to these types of questions will provide you with the path you need to follow in order to create the best succession plan for your organization. This part helps you anticipate and overcome obstacles you may encounter along the way, and equips you with the tools you need to evaluate the success of your plan.

Chapter 4

Preparing the Plan: Six Steps to Success(ion)

*Y*ou're ready to develop a succession plan. Now, how the heck do you go about preparing it? Like other operations in your organization, preparing a succession plan is a systematic process.

It begins with determining what type of plan you need, selecting planning team members, and identifying any factors that will influence the plan (such as current talent mix, potential sources of key employees, and labor market conditions).

Next, you need to spell out the plan's ingredients, list actions to be taken by whom in what time frame, and describe how those actions link to your overall strategic plan. You also need to identify talent sources available to fill succession vacancies.

Finally, you need to determine how you'll communicate the plan, both in writing and in presentations, and how the team will get the commitment of various personnel to ensure the plan's success.

At first blush, this process may seem very complex, but it really isn't. It all boils down to a systematic, simple, six-step process. In this chapter, I describe these six steps and offer tips and guidelines for helping you successfully construct a viable succession plan — a plan that is tailored to your organization.

Step 1: Figuring Out What Type of Plan You Need

You need to start with a clear understanding of the type of succession plan you're constructing. The type of plan you identify will determine the following:

- The size of your planning team
- Who you select to be team members
- The role that HR plays in developing the plan
- Which key positions you include
- How you look at market trends
- The scope of your plan
- The time frame of your plan
- How your succession plan fits into your organization's overall strategic plan
- The talent sources you decide to tap

There are essentially three types of succession plans (see Chapter 3 for more information):

- Plans that deal with unexpected departures
- Plans that ensure smooth and orderly, predictable transitions
- Longer-range, strategic succession plans

Some companies experience higher turnover than others, some are growing more rapidly then planned, some have many workers who will be retiring in the next few years, some are expanding their product or service offering. Whatever the case may be, there's a succession plan that will suit your needs.

You can determine which of the three types of succession plans you need to prepare by asking yourself why you need a succession plan.

Are you facing unexpected departures?

Unexpected departures can occur for a number of reasons:

- Death
- Illness requiring temporary absence

✔ Illness resulting in a disability

✔ Family crisis

✔ Resignation to take another job

✔ Termination due to wrongful conduct

If unexpected departures are your primary concern, or if you've already experienced one of these events, it's time for you to develop the first type of succession plan: an unexpected-departure succession plan to ensure that you won't be caught off-guard in the future.

Are you thinking about planned departures?

Every organization deals with the planned transition of an important talent from time to time:

✔ A manager plans retirement.

✔ An employee with a needed special talent is temporarily assigned to another office to help solve a problem.

✔ After years of hard work, a key talent plans an extensive vacation.

✔ A talented individual is preparing for a promotion to another position.

If you know an important employee is planning to leave, you need the second type of succession plan: a predictable-departure succession plan.

Are you thinking strategically?

You're observing the rapidly changing marketplace and thinking long-term. You're assessing your personnel strengths to meet current and potential future challenges. You want to develop a succession plan that ensures your organization will be ready for anything.

What you need is a long-term, strategic succession plan, a plan that develops current talent and anticipates potential talent needed to pursue your organizational vision in the future. Although the other two types of plans should be congruent with your strategic plan, this type of plan is more fully integrated with and focused on your organization's overall strategic plan.

Step 2: Forming Your Planning Team

Picking the right balance of people for your succession-planning team is critical to the success of your plan. This team will be responsible for determining the plan's scope, the key positions to be included, and where and how potential talent will be found.

The following sections discuss how to select the right members for your planning team and how to make sure everyone works together successfully.

Selecting the right team members

Selecting the right team members is very important. You need people who are knowledgeable about the talent involved in your plan, people who are good at mapping out processes, people who are good communicators, and people who are connected and respected in the organization in ways that will enable them to gain widespread commitment to the plan after it's communicated.

Here are some helpful suggestions for the kinds of people you should look for to become members of your succession-planning team:

- ✔ **Select someone who represents or communicates to top management.** The support of top management for the succession plan is essential.

- ✔ **Put more emphasis on selecting people you know will work effectively together as a team than on their job titles.**

- ✔ **Select people who are open to diverse viewpoints.**

- ✔ **Make sure that HR is represented on your team.** HR will play an important role in implementing your finished plan.

- ✔ **For an unexpected-departure succession plan, be sure to select people who are available for and capable of rapid response.**

- ✔ **If you're developing an unexpected-departure succession plan, make sure you have a team member who is familiar with the needed competencies of the departing talent.** This person may be a key manager, a key technical talent, or someone in another important position.

- ✔ **For a strategic succession plan, select people who are familiar with your organization's overall strategic plan and knowledgeable about the kind of talent needed to achieve your organizational mission.**

Establishing an effective team climate

Some people are more experienced at working on teams than others. After you've selected the team members, make sure that they know about, agree to, and practice the following set of behaviors that characterize an effective team climate:

- ✔ Everyone focuses on the common goal of developing an effective plan.

- ✔ Everyone respects and trusts each other.

- ✔ No one tries to dominate other people.

- ✔ Communication among team members is open and widespread.

- ✔ Team members feel free to express their feelings, ideas, and opinions.

- ✔ Conflict and disagreement among team members is focused primarily on the ideas offered when solving problems, not on proving other people wrong.

- ✔ Everyone recognizes that the team members need each other.

- ✔ Team members actively collaborate and help each other.

- ✔ Team members self-initiate action toward the team's shared purpose, without waiting for someone to direct them.

- ✔ Everyone accepts assignments with enthusiasm.

- ✔ No one is preoccupied with individual status and position.

Figuring out who does what

After team members have been selected and the team climate has been established, the team figures out who will play what role. Ideally, HR should play the leading role because they're responsible for ensuring that your organization has the right leadership and talent to accomplish its mission.

Here are some questions that need to be addressed when you're figuring out who does what on the team:

- ✔ **Who will be responsible for identifying potentially vulnerable positions (positions that you may need to fill sooner rather than later)?**

- ✔ **Who will responsible for identifying the competencies needed?**

- ✔ **Who will be responsible for carrying out any talent search required by the plan?**

- ✔ **Who will be responsible for writing the plan so it can be distributed to the appropriate people?** After the plan is completed, it must be clearly written as a formal succession plan.

- ✔ **Who will be responsible for coordinating and delivering a communication strategy?** After the plan is completed, it must be communicated throughout the organization.

- ✔ **Who will be responsible for monitoring, evaluating, and adjusting the plan after it's implemented?**

Step 3: Determining What Factors Will Influence Your Plan

A successful succession plan must anticipate many factors that will influence the plan. Are trends in the marketplace requiring new kinds of talent? Are there major changes in the sources of talent pools? What is the effect of changing generational and diverse cultural populations?

Trends in the marketplace

The marketplace is changing every day. Financial pressures are shaping organizational decisions and customer buying habits. Cultural diversity is growing at an ascending rate. Younger generations are populating the marketplace. The result is a variety of changing customer needs.

How do changes in the marketplace affect your succession plan? They require you to determine what kinds of talent you need in your organization to effectively deal with the changes. They also call for you to make sure that you have the talent you need to deal with the changes.

What kinds of questions should your planning team be asking to deal with the changing marketplace? Here are some examples:

- ✔ How are customer buying habits changing?

- ✔ What role is the Internet playing in shaping customer behaviors?

- ✔ How are customer expectations changing?

- ✔ How are customer needs changing?

> ✔ What kinds of competition have emerged and how much?
>
> ✔ To what extent has globalization affected your organization?

The succession-planning team needs to ask, answer, and discuss these kinds of questions as you develop an effective succession plan.

Although these questions are important to an unexpected-departure succession plan and a predictable-departure succession plan, they're critically important to a strategic succession plan.

During the planning process, team members must be aware of the influence of the changing marketplace on every decision they make. Answering these questions will influence the kinds of talent that your organization needs. For example, in discussing answers to the first question, the team may note that more and more customers are buying online, which calls for more technical talent.

Changes in talent pools

Another influence on succession planning is the quality, diversity, and availability of required talent pools. Many factors are shaping and changing talent pools:

✔ The globalization of organizations, requiring new kinds of leadership

✔ Advances in technology, requiring new kinds of talent

✔ A more educated workforce

✔ The increasing use of outsourcing as a source of talent

✔ A shrinking talent pool due to increased competition

✔ More experienced talent due to lower retention levels

✔ Impending retirement of large numbers of skilled and experienced Baby Boomers.

Team members must be aware of changes taking place in talent pools. Those changes will affect not only what kind of talent is available, but also how that talent should be managed and developed after being hired.

Generational and cultural diversity

Still another influence on your succession plan is the increase in generational and cultural diversity. People are living longer and retiring later in their lives. Meanwhile, the younger generation, typically referred to as the *Millennial Generation,* is increasing its presence in the workplace.

The mixture of generations in the workplace is greater than ever before in our history, from Baby Boomers to Gen Xers to Millennials. Each generation is a product of its time, coming into the workplace with its own set of motivations, expectations, attitudes, and demands from the organization:

- ✔ **Baby Boomers:** Baby Boomers (people born between 1946 and 1964 or so) were raised to respect authority figures. They were raised with a sense of optimism and a feeling that they're a special generation, capable of changing the world. They define their self-worth by their work — in fact, Baby Boomers have been credited with coining the term *workaholic*. They believe that hard work and sacrifice is the price they have to pay for becoming successful. Boomers are goal oriented, confident, and competent at completing tasks assigned to them. They're reluctant to disagree with peers. They value the chain of command and respect authority.

- ✔ **Generation X:** Gen Xers (people born between 1965 and 1980 or so) are also good task completers. They're independent and self-reliant. They want their achievements to be recognized. Gen Xers value personal growth and personal gratification. They thrive on the possibility of change. Like Baby Boomers, they value the chain of command. More than previous generations, they seek a balance between their work and personal lives. They have strong feelings of loyalty toward their family and friends.

- ✔ **Millennials:** The Millennial Generation (those born between 1980 and the late 1990s or so) is the most educated generation. They're very comfortable with technology. They value collaboration and teamwork. They accept and value diversity. Millennials are very flexible and adaptable to change. They're multi-taskers, confident, and optimistic. They value training.

Meanwhile, businesses are going more global and society has become more culturally diverse. This diversity has opened up organizations to new pools of talent with differences in viewpoints, expectations at work, connections to social networks, and cultural understanding of businesses in today's world.

When it comes to succession planning, especially strategic succession planning, your planning team has to consider the resulting talents and associated behaviors springing from this diversity. For example, if your organization is growing globally, a culturally diverse talent pool is more valuable to you, because it will bring you a greater understanding of and ability to effectively operate in different cultures.

Step 4: Linking Your Succession Plan to Your Strategic Plan

No matter what type of succession plan you're developing, it must fit with and support your overall strategic plan. An organization's strategic plan tells people what the organization is all about. It tells people something about the origin and history of the organization, how it's functioning at the present time, and what aspirations it has for the future.

Aligning the succession plan to your vision, mission, and strategies

To align your succession plan to your vision, mission, and strategies, being able to distinguish between them is helpful:

- ✔ **Vision:** An organizational *vision* is essentially a snapshot of the future, a picture of what you want your organization to look like and where you want it to go in the future. It sets expectations for employees and identifies your intended customer base.

- ✔ **Mission statement:** Your organizational *mission statement* is more focused on the here and now. It turns the vision into a primary goal and supporting objectives. It establishes the criteria for defining the competencies you need in various organizational positions. The mission statement is a standard for measuring your organization's success.

- ✔ **Strategies:** Overall, your *strategies* are like a long-range map or set of instructions and processes for how you'll achieve your organizational mission and realize your vision. As such, your strategies are a kind of guiding light for decisions made and actions taken. This includes succession planning.

No matter what type of succession plan you're developing, it must fit with and support your organization's overall strategic plan. For example, when you're replacing a top executive, the values, aspirations, talents, and competencies of the new hire must support your organization's strategic plan. When you're replacing a key talent, such as an engineer or sales manager, again, the values, aspirations, talents, and competencies of the new hire must support your organization's strategic plan.

Partnering with HR

Unfortunately, many businesses don't fully involve HR in the development of their strategic plans. Hopefully, that isn't the case with your organization.

In order to best serve your organization, make sure that your HR department is thoroughly familiar with your organization's overall strategic plan — your business and where it's going. Only then can HR be a valuable resource for needed talent and expertise. Then be sure to fully involve HR in the development of your succession plan.

Involving HR is critical to the success of your succession plan. Why? For a number of reasons:

- ✔ **The HR department coordinates selection and staffing of personnel for the organization.** Members of the department, therefore, need to be aware of any staffing needs called for by the succession plan.

- ✔ **HR's job is to know where to find the right people for each position.** To do that, HR needs to be informed of the personnel needs specified in the succession plan.

- ✔ **When they're knowledgeable about the long-range strategic plan, HR personnel can help the strategic planning team project future staffing and employment needs.**

- ✔ **The HR department oversees training and development in the organization.** Knowing the competencies and talents required to fill the vacancy specified by the succession plan enables HR to train and develop new hires, helping them blend into the organization.

- ✔ **The HR department coordinates *organizational development,* the systems and processes of the organization.** Knowing the organization systems and processes and what kind of competencies and talent fit them gives HR a perspective on the organization that helps the succession-planning team identify needed people.

Identifying positions that need to be filled

Here's where identifying the type of plan (as you did in Step 1) becomes important.

- ✔ **Are you looking for someone to immediately fill a position left vacant due to an unexpected departure?** If you haven't already prepared for such a crisis, you'll have to move very quickly. This situation also should stimulate you to set up an unexpected-departure succession plan for the future.

✔ **Are you aware of one or more predictable departures of key people due to retirement, planned hospitalizations, promotions, relocations, and so on?** You have a little more time to develop a predictable-departure succession plan. However, here again, if you don't already have a transition plan in place, construct one to also serve future potential departures.

✔ **Are you updating your strategic plan due to new innovations, customer demands, or market trends?** In updating your strategic plan, what do you anticipate your organization will need in terms of skills, expertise, experience, and talent? The long-range, strategic succession plan will be revised in the future as the organization's overall strategic plan is adjusted.

Whichever type of plan you're working on and whatever positions you've identified as needing to be filled, you have to know where to find the needed candidates.

Step 5: Identifying Potential Candidate Sources

Based on your identification of the needed candidates, you need to describe the competency required for the position to be filled.

Identifying needed competencies

Competency is the characteristics and behaviors of a person that lead him or her to perform a job successfully. A person's competencies may be derived from or based on his or her knowledge, skills, experience, or just plain natural talent.

To determine the competencies you need in a candidate for the position you need to fill, ask the following questions:

✔ **What kinds of information and expertise should the candidate possess to effectively perform the job?** For example, a broad knowledge about techniques of persuasion would be invaluable to a sales trainer.

✔ **What particular skill or set of skills should the candidate possess to effectively perform the job?** For example, being skilled at writing and clearly communicating an idea or concept would be necessary for a marketing director.

✔ **What kinds of experience should the candidate possess to effectively perform the job?** For example, a lawyer with extensive experience in corporate law may be a good candidate to head your legal department.

✔ **What kinds of *natural talents* (behaviors that easily occur without any thought or practice) do you need in a potential candidate?** For example, a person who is just naturally a people person may be an excellent candidate for a key position in your public-relations department.

The competency you need in a candidate may be knowledge, skills, experience, talent, or a combination of these things. After you have identified and can describe the needed competencies, you're ready to look for what you need.

For a more detailed discussion of competencies, see Chapter 9.

Developing a list of internal potentials

One of the first places to look for potential candidates is in your own backyard. You may find that people currently working in your organization have just the right set of competencies for the job that you need to fill. This is where the HR department plays a very important role on your succession-planning team.

After you've defined the candidate competencies needed, HR can construct a job and then be able to identify potential internal sources to fill it by

✔ Posting job descriptions

✔ Tapping into organizational job description databases to locate potential candidates

✔ Identifying qualified people who are ready to be promoted, based on a review of their career paths, formal and informal training, and performance evaluations

✔ Identifying qualified employees who can easily transfer from another job in your organization

Another internal source of potential candidates is suggestions from current or former employees. In addition to being able to refer someone, a current employee knows enough about the organization to judge whether a person would be a good fit. You can be confident that employees will make what they think are good recommendations, because they won't want to be embarrassed by a poor choice. A side benefit of this internal source is that it's cost-effective.

Still another "quasi-internal" source is re-recruiting former employees and job applicants. In both cases, HR already knows something about the potential candidates and may be able to suggest people who will fit.

Compiling external sources of talent

In today's highly connected work world, a great variety of external sources of talent exist:

- ✔ **Online:** Due to the explosive growth of computer technology, there are many sources of potential candidates on the Internet:
    - There are numerous job boards, such as Monster (www. monster.com), on which employers can post job descriptions or search for candidates.
    - There are sites that compile lists of job board sites, such as www.newcanaancats.org/job_boards_list. htm.
    - Websites of professional associations, such as the American Society for Training and Development (www.astd.org), often have an employment section. Depending on the position to be filled, these websites can be more targeted, saving you a great deal of time.
    - You can post your job needs on your organization's website.
- ✔ **Employment agencies and search firms:** These firms will do some preliminary screening for you and put you in touch with applicants for a fee. Search firms typically charge a fee for finding and delivering potentially suitable candidates to your firm, whereas employment agencies tend to charge a fee only if you hire the individual they refer.
- ✔ **Colleges and universities:** For jobs that require a college degree, particularly in technical areas, colleges and universities are a potential source for candidates. The downside is that they're an expensive place to recruit, due to travel costs, hours spent arranging and coordinating visits, and setting up for visits.
- ✔ **Job fairs:** Setting up or attending existing job fairs can be a very efficient method for finding talent at a variety of levels.

Training to develop needed talent

Typically, in any organization, there are people with competencies that could be further developed with training and coaching to match what the organization needs. Guided by the organization's overall strategic plan, many HR departments have established talent development programs to accomplish that goal. These programs provide another internal source of talent.

Your HR department has the employee data to be able to identify potential candidates who, with some additional training, could be prepared to fill the position you're looking for. Use that data.

For much more information on the development of needed talent, see Chapter 10.

Step 6: Putting It All Together

The first five steps in succession planning give you the most important ingredients of a succession plan. Now you're ready to pull all those ingredients together into a coherent step-by-step plan.

Establishing your goals

Putting everything together begins as most planning does, with establishing the goals of your plan. The goals of your plan are a function of the position you need to fill — pure and simple.

- ✔ Are you needing to fill a vacancy caused by the abrupt departure of an important manager or other critical talent?

- ✔ Are you needing to plan for the potential departure of someone you know is planning to retire, to move, and so on?

- ✔ Are you looking at market challenges and realizing that replacing departing talent may require new competencies to meet the challenges?

The goal of your plan may be very narrowly targeted to a specific position or it may be a multi-goal plan to meet your organizational needs as your organization moves strategically to accomplish your mission and realize your vision.

Regardless, your goal must be clearly stated so that you can measure your plan's success.

Describing the process steps

Given the goal of your succession plan, you're now ready to describe the specific steps that you must carry out. These steps may be very simple and straightforward or more complex, depending on the goal of your succession plan.

Although the following sample steps illustrate what you may include in a longer-range, comprehensive succession plan that anticipates both present and future personnel needs, its basic components are needed in any succession plan:

1. **Identify which positions need to be filled immediately or in the near future.**

2. **Identify potential staffing needs, given changes in your strategic plan or challenges in the marketplace.**

3. **Identify the competencies needed for each position.**

4. **Determine where candidates with the needed competencies can be found.**

   Specify both internal and external sources of potential candidates.

5. **Interview and assess potential candidates to determine their fit for the needed position or positions.**

6. **Hire and orient the selected candidates.**

Specifying a timeline

As in any plan, establishing a timeline and who is responsible for the completion of each step is important.

Figure 4-1 shows an example timeline for hiring a bakery operations director to work in a grocery store market chain.

Notice in this example that some of the activities overlap. It's entirely possible, for example, that interested candidates will be identified within two weeks after the job has been posted and advertised. The key consideration is the endpoints of the activities — they're the targeted dates for completing each phase of the process.

Communicating the plan

You've completed the drafting of the succession plan. Now comes a very important step, a step that some people don't give enough attention to: communicating your succession plan.

SUCCESSION PLAN FOR OPERATIONS DIRECTOR RETIRING JUNE 15

1. Determine job competencies and write job description.

						WHO IS RESPONSIBLE?
JAN	FEB	MAR	APR	MAY	JUN	John and Alex

FEB 15

2. Identify candidate sources and post/advertise the job description.

						WHO IS RESPONSIBLE?
JAN	FEB	MAR	APR	MAY	JUN	Alex

FEB 1   MAY 1

3. Interview candidates.

						WHO IS RESPONSIBLE?
JAN	FEB	MAR	APR	MAY	JUN	John, Alex, & Jessica

MAR 1   MAY 20

4. Select candidate and make offer.

						WHO IS RESPONSIBLE?
JAN	FEB	MAR	APR	MAY	JUN	John

MAY 20   JUN 15

5. New Operations Director is hired, oriented, and begins work.

						WHO IS RESPONSIBLE?
JAN	FEB	MAR	APR	MAY	JUN	John and Jessica

JUN 15

Figure 4-1: A timeline helps ensure that your plan is on track.

The process of communicating your succession plan is important for a variety of reasons:

✔ **Developing a succession plan behind closed doors and not communicating it adequately can lead to some very disturbing rumors.** In this day and age of globalization and economic uncertainty, any rumor floating around the organization can make people feel insecure. People want to feel secure in their jobs. They want to know what's happening and how it will affect them.

✔ **In recent decades there has been a growing trend toward empowering employees, fostering a sense of their importance to the organization.** The more openly managers communicate to employees and inform them what's going on, the more employees will feel that they're an important part of the organization.

✔ **In any succession plan, candidates often are selected from within the organization.** Knowing that there may be opportunities for advancement or movement to another key position in the organization when a vacancy occurs helps people feel more committed to the organization and its future. They'll know that the plan isn't just another bureaucratic activity, but something that offers them a potential opportunity.

> ✔ **By communicating your plan openly, positively, and with a sense of inclusiveness you'll establish a foundation for getting the commitment of people throughout the organization, which is necessary for it to succeed.**

Depending on the size of your organization, there are many possible ways to communicate your plan:

- ✔ Begin by communicating the plan to key managers to gain their commitment.

- ✔ Bring everyone together in a meeting to present and discuss the plan if your organization isn't too large. This makes it more personal to everyone. Present and discuss your plan in department meetings if your organization is larger.

- ✔ If you have an employee newsletter, include a column from the CEO, positively describing the overall purpose and processes of the succession plan and emphasizing that the organization is open to considering internal candidates.

- ✔ Use e-mail to distribute your plan to everyone.

 No matter which method you use for communicating your plan, make sure you invite people to offer comments and even ask questions, which, of course, you'll answer. Also, make sure that you communicate your plan in a positive, exciting, and inclusive manner. Your goal is to show people how your succession plan will make the organization more viable and stable.

Now What?

 You've constructed a plan. You've covered all six steps, and you're ready to implement your plan. Here are a few thoughts to keep in mind as you proceed:

- ✔ **Don't stop here.** Yes, you have a plan. Now, stick to it! Make sure it keeps being a priority. After all, steady succession of key talent leads to the sustainability of your organizational success.

- ✔ **Be ready for change.** As the old saying goes, "Change is the only constant." You may have a wonderfully complete plan, but be alert to forces that may require you to alter it — the changing marketplace, changing talent pools, new product innovations requiring different talent, new competition, and so on.

- ✔ **Maintain your plan's visibility in your organization.** People who are informed and know where they're going will feel more involved and more satisfied in your workplace.

Chapter 5

Implementing the Plan

· ·

In This Chapter

▶ Laying the groundwork for a successful launch

▶ Getting support from your plan within your organization

▶ Meeting the challenges of a launch

▶ Getting better every time

· ·

You and your colleagues have spent countless hours in many meetings developing a succession plan, but, finally, you have it, and it's ready to be implemented.

Even the best plan in the world won't do you any good if you don't implement it effectively. To accomplish the goals you have for your succession plan, your plan's implementation must be clearly communicated, supported by key people within your organization, and executed without a hitch.

In this chapter, I walk you through how to implement the succession plan you've worked so hard to create. I end the chapter by offering some suggestions for how to improve future implementations of your plan. Mistakes are bound to happen, so you need to seize the opportunity to learn from those mistakes.

Collecting Baseline Data

Before you implement your new succession plan, take the time to collect some *baseline data* — data showing how your organization is performing *before* the plan is implemented. This baseline data will be important when you're evaluating the success of the plan down the road (see Chapter 6).

Before you implement your succession plan, you may want to ask the following:

- ✔ How long does it take your organization to find and hire candidates to replace key employees?

- ✔ What percentage of vacancies in key positions are you able to fill?

- ✔ How many vacant positions do you fill in a set time period (for example, the six-month period before the plan is implemented)?

- ✔ How many people have you identified and developed within your organization to prepare them to fill vacant positions?

- ✔ What's the ratio of the number of people recruited from within your organization to the number of people recruited from external sources?

Only by comparing the numbers *before* you implement your succession plan to the numbers *after* you implement your succession plan will you be able to draw conclusions about your plan's success.

Starting Off on the Right Foot

When you're ready to start implementing your succession plan, you need to make sure that it starts off on the right foot. You do that by sharing it with people in your organization, particularly the key people you need to support it. In this section, I walk you through how to present your succession plan so that it has the best possible chance of succeeding.

Circulating a formal version of your plan

The first step is to prepare a step-by-step written version of your succession plan for circulation within your organization. The document must be clearly written so that people can quickly understand what needs to be done.

Here are some general guidelines to keep in mind:

- ✔ **Write succinctly.** Avoid long, complicated sentences as much as possible. Write short paragraphs, not long or rambling ones.

- ✔ **Use numbered or bulleted lists to clearly portray the steps you're describing or points you want to make.** Not sure when to use numbers versus bullets? Here's a tip: Use numbered lists when you're communicating steps that must be followed in a particular order; use bulleted lists when the order doesn't matter.

✔ **Avoid highly technical or excessive legal language.** Unless you're absolutely sure that such language is necessary and will be familiar to your audience, eliminate the jargon.

✔ **Wherever possible, use a table or a diagram to convey information.** Many people are visual, and tables or diagrams make it easier for them to comprehend what you're planning.

In addition to these stylistic tips (which you can apply in just about any written document, by the way), remember the following guidelines when you're putting together your succession plan:

✔ **Begin your plan by describing why you need it.** Why is the succession plan important to your organization?

✔ **Be sure to tie your succession plan to your organization's overall strategic plan.** Make it clear how your succession plan will contribute to the achievement of your organizational mission.

✔ **Clearly state the goals of your plan.** More important, state them in terms of measurable objectives.

✔ **Lay out a series of tasks that will have to be completed to achieve those goals and describe the steps that will be taken for each task.** Establish specific timelines for completing each task. Identify the people who will be involved in carrying out each task, and the person responsible for making sure each task gets done.

✔ **Design and implement a procedure that will help you get feedback as you monitor and adjust your plan.**

After you've put together a written version of your succession plan, you're ready to circulate it to all the people involved in the plan and any other key people whose support you'll need.

Preparing presentations

After your written succession plan starts making the rounds in your organization, you'll be meeting with managers or other employee groups to describe and discuss the plan. So, as soon as you've written your comprehensive succession-planning document (see the preceding section), you need to prepare brief presentations that you can use in those meetings.

In particular, you should prepare the following:

- ✔ **A generic version of the presentation that you can use with any group of people in your organization to give them a sense of your plan:** This presentation should provide a good general overview of the plan.

- ✔ **One or more specialized presentations that cover segments of the plan aimed at particular parts of your organization:** For example, if you're dealing with an IT department, your presentation should describe the parts of your plan that deal with key talent in that department.

Keep your presentations short and to the point. Include enough detail to cover what you want to convey without overwhelming meeting participants. Include a way for people to give you feedback and suggestions for possible revisions.

The important role of HR

In both your formal succession plan and the presentations you give about it, be sure to emphasize the role that HR will play in implementing the plan.

Your organization may be small, with only one or two people performing the HR functions. Or it may be a larger organization with a full-fledged HR staff. Regardless, HR will be responsible for carrying out many (if not most) of the steps in the succession process. The HR staff does all the following:

- ✔ Helps your organization identify what talents and competencies you'll need in the next year, two years, or ten years

- ✔ Identifies key people in your organization, people whose absence would damage the productivity and/or quality of what you provide customers

- ✔ Researches and identifies the competencies needed to fill key positions

- ✔ Identifies talent pools and recruitment sources for new hires

- ✔ Maintains a base of current competencies and skills, identifies and tracks the training and development of internal talent, and has a departmental as well as companywide view of people who are potential candidates for vacant key positions

- ✔ Interviews, screens, and finalizes the hiring of needed people

- ✔ Orients and provides the necessary support and training to new hires to help them smoothly transition into the organization

HR is an important strategic force, an essential agent in achieving the goals of your succession plan. So, as you distribute and communicate your plan, make sure you emphasize the important role of HR.

Garnering Broad Support for Your Plan

Your succession plan won't succeed if it doesn't have the support of top management. The CEO and his or her top managers must be fully behind it.

Ideally, your top management has been involved in the succession-planning process from the beginning, is fully aware of its details, and is strongly championing the plan. But if this isn't the case, here are some steps you can take:

✔ **If you have a board of directors, share the plan with them.** Make sure they support it completely. Make their support visible to the entire organization, using announcements posted on bulletin boards, mass e-mail messages, articles in an employee newsletter, and so on.

✔ **Circulate your written copy of the plan to your CEO and top managers.** Ask them to review the plan by a specified date and set up a meeting to discuss the plan with them. When you meet, listen to any last-minute suggestions they have for revising the plan to make it more effective. Make sure management is familiar enough with the plan that they can answer any questions they may face about it down the road. Get them to pledge their support for your plan in their meetings, at publicity events, and anytime an employee asks about it.

✔ **Share the presentations you created with department managers to make sure they're familiar with the succession plan.** Discuss ways they could be helpful in the implementation of your plan. In concert with department managers, schedule department meetings for them to personally share the succession plan with their employees. Letting employees know how much you're thinking ahead is a signal to them that you're enhancing their job security and stability, as well as moving the organization forward.

At some point, the implementation of your succession plan will be relevant to and/or involve employees at different levels, so the more visibly management supports it, the fewer internal obstacles you'll run into during the implementation process.

At first, communicating the plan to all the top managers, department managers, and employees in various departments may seem like a lot of unnecessary work. But doing so will yield several important benefits:

✔ It gives employees a glimpse into your organization's future and will help them see that they're an important part of your organization. This, in turn, will stimulate them to give their support to your plan whenever needed.

✔ It helps employees see their own potential opportunities for development and advancement within the organization. This, in turn, will stimulate them to feel more motivated and less likely to consider opportunities in other organizations.

✔ The overall potential benefit of all this is higher morale and increased loyalty to your organization.

In some ways, sharing your succession plan with employees is an opportunity to use it as a kind of team-building strategy. It focuses their attention on your organization's long-term strategy and highlights their interdependence — the connected role they all play in achieving your organization's mission. Instead of seeing themselves as just doing their jobs, they'll see that they're important parts of the organization.

Meeting Challenges Head On

Your succession plan is clearly defined. It's fully supported. It's visible throughout your organization. Now you're ready to launch it.

You've already taken a huge step by drafting a succession plan and garnering support for the plan in your organization. But when you set about recruiting and selecting replacement candidates, you're bound to come upon some hurdles. In this section, I walk you through some of the most common challenges that come in implementing a succession plan, and give you strategies for overcoming these challenges to meet your goal.

Recruiting external talent

Recruiting candidates to replace departing people is an essential step in the implementation of any succession plan. Inevitably, you'll run into some challenges when implementing this step, but they don't have to derail you.

In this section, I cover some of the most likely challenges you could encounter and tips for minimizing them quickly, or even preventing them from occurring in the first place.

One predominant theme runs through all these tips: Be flexible. As you implement any plan — whether it's a succession plan or some other plan in your organization — you'll frequently have to adjust your expectations and make changes. If you're flexible, you'll improve your chances of meeting your goal.

Limited time

Recruiting good people takes time. As you implement the recruitment step of your succession plan, don't be impatient. Give it the time needed for you to feel confident that you've tapped as many candidate sources as possible. Depending on the talent pools available to you, this could take several weeks.

 During the implementation, track the effectiveness of the various recruitment resources and strategies that you're using, and be flexible enough to adjust your timeline if necessary.

 If your recruitment process takes *too* much time, you may lose some applicants to other organizations. *Remember:* Applicants probably aren't applying only for your opening — if they're looking for a job, they're blanketing the universe with their résumés. Make sure that your procedures are streamlined enough that you don't keep applicants hanging.

An inadequate or out-of-date job description

This kind of problem will most likely occur when you have an ongoing succession-planning process already in place that team members regard as complete. To protect against this, make sure that your plan includes specific processes for periodically updating job descriptions.

 In this stage of the recruitment process, you must have a clear understanding of the responsibilities of the person who will fill the open position, as well as specific information regarding the knowledge, experience, and competencies needed to successfully perform in that role.

A lack of qualified candidates

You may have a lack of qualified candidates for a number of reasons:

- ✔ **Maybe your job opening wasn't marketed well.** You may discover that your job announcement wasn't detailed enough, stated clearly enough, or distributed in the right places. Make sure as you implement this step that you're covering all your bases by reviewing the broad range of online and offline recruitment sources that are available today.

✔ **Maybe you've made changes to your strategic plan that are pulling your organization in a new direction, but there aren't many people who can fill the position you're trying to fill to achieve your revised mission.** Be ready to offer any needed training to help existing people adjust to the new plan. You may even have to hire additional people with the right qualifications.

✔ **Maybe the kind of person you're looking for is rare.** The more specialized the talent, the more likely this situation is, particularly in a depressed economy (see the next bullet). You may be forced to change your timeline in order to implement a longer search. Again, allow yourself the flexibility to change timelines when needed as you implement your plan.

✔ **Maybe a depressed economy is pressuring candidates to stay where they already are, secure and comfortable in their current jobs.** Your only choice in this situation is to make sure that the opportunity you're offering candidates is more attractive. You may need to increase the salary, improve the benefits, or offer long-range stability (in the form of a contract that guarantees employment for a set amount of time) to lure the right candidates to your organization.

✔ **Maybe your competition in the marketplace is attracting the very kinds of candidates you're looking for.** Again, your only choice is to make your position more attractive in any way you can, especially in terms of salary, benefits, and long-range stability.

If the compensation you're offering isn't competitive in the marketplace, you have a decision to make: Do you raise the salary, or stick to your guns and keep looking? Beware of short-term thinking. Adjusting compensation, even if it requires other sacrifices in the short term, may help you find the person you need — and that person will be worth the higher compensation in the long run.

A large volume of applicants

You may find yourself overwhelmed by a large number of applicants, particularly if the unemployment rate is high. On the one hand, having an abundance of applicants can be a blessing. On the other, it could overwhelm your recruitment process.

If you anticipate getting a large number of applicants for a position, given your current economic climate, assign someone to help weed through the applications. Adjust your timelines to allow ample opportunity to accomplish this task.

Complex application formats

In today's increasingly technological world, you may find yourself handling a wide variety of different job-application formats, such as differing forms from various recruitment agencies, e-mail requests and applications, faxed résumés, and applications delivered by regular mail. As you implement your succession plan, make sure that you've designed efficient and detailed processes for directing people how to handle these variations.

Incomplete data

Because of the different forms used by different candidate sources, you may not get all the data you want for a particular candidate. You can prevent this from happening by making sure that you provide each talent source with a description of exactly the kinds of information you need before they send in any candidate possibilities.

A complicated recruitment process

Even though the recruitment process you set up as you developed your succession plan may have seemed efficient at the time, as you implement the plan, you may suddenly find it to be too complicated. Your recruitment process may have too many steps or too much red tape.

If you're getting the sense that the recruitment process is too complicated, your succession-planning team needs to be flexible and ready to change it as needed, to minimize its complexity.

Recruiting internal talent

Whether you're looking to fill a top management position or some other key position in the organization, your succession plan is very likely to have a component focusing on the identification and development of internal talent.

One of the most frustrating things that can happen in the heat of implementation is discovering that you don't have an adequate supply of internal talent. If that happens:

- ✔ **Immediately take actions to expand your talent pool.** You communicated your plan to top managers and department heads during management meetings in preparation for launching your plan. Now, go back to those managers and get their help in identifying potential candidates.

- ✔ **Quickly spread the word throughout your organization, describing the particular kind of talent you urgently need and asking them for recommendations.** Even though you may have an active internal development program in place, you may be surprised to find that some people have been missed in the process.

You may discover that the identified internal talent hasn't been developed as much as needed for the position you're trying to fill. Here, you face some choices:

- ✔ If you have enough time, immediately provide appropriate training and coaching to bring the person up to speed.

- ✔ If your need is urgent and you don't have time to bring someone up to speed, consider conditionally moving the identified talent into the position and providing him or her with immediate, ongoing training, coaching, and mentoring for a trial period. In the meantime, just in case it doesn't work out, continue searching for talent.

- ✔ If all else fails, switch your search to external talent sources to find the talent you need.

For a more detailed discussion of the role of internal talent development during succession planning, see Chapter 10.

Promotion is a special case of internal talent. It's different from development in that not all people developed move upward in the organization; in many cases, they may make a lateral move to another key position.

Promoting someone from within to fill a vacancy can be very beneficial to an organization. It signals to people that you're open to their career development with opportunities for advancement in the future. And this can only help increase their motivation, as well as their loyalty and enthusiasm for the organization.

However, promotion isn't without its challenges, so keep the following cautions in mind:

- ✔ **Be very careful when selecting someone to promote to the vacant position.** Someone's performance in his or her current job may not be a good predictor of performance in the new job. The knowledge, competencies, and talents needed may be different. For example, a highly successful salesperson who seems to get along with everyone may not have the complex competencies needed by a sales manager. Make sure you pay very close attention to the profile you developed for the vacant position during your succession-planning process before you promote someone.

- ✔ **When you promote someone to a vacant position, don't forget about the vacancy you're creating elsewhere.** Make sure you've done the work necessary to fill the newly vacant position before you promote someone.

✔ **Before you promote someone from one area to another area in the organization, be sure he or she will fit into the new subculture.** Over time, every department or section of an organization develops its own little subculture — its own values, norms, and ways of doing things.

✔ **Check with people in the candidate's area before you officially promote him or her.** You wouldn't want to promote someone who has developed a negative reputation for one reason or another — for example, being critical of colleagues or not being able to work effectively as a team member.

✔ **If you find yourself selecting a person who has been competing with several other people who want to be promoted, keep in mind that this could affect the morale of the people who don't get the job.** When promoting someone, spend some time meeting with the people you didn't select, clearly defining the reasons why you decided to go another way. Being open and spelling out the criteria that you use, could help them to get a promotion the next time around.

Making a decision

One of the most critical events when implementing your succession plan is making a selection decision. Making a bad decision can be very costly in terms of time, money, productivity, morale, and so on. So, you need to ensure that the decision you make is a good one.

You may put candidates through a rigorous screening process and an intensive background check, and subject them to a series of tests, such as personality tests or simulations. Sifting through all that data to draw conclusions will help you make your selection decision, but it's a time-consuming process. Make sure you allocate enough resources to this component of the selection process. Such data gives you important information to help you arrive at your selection decision.

Even more important than data is the face-to-face interview process, during which you not only gather more information about the candidate, but also form impressions about his or her values, attitudes, behaviors, and a sense of how well he or she will fit into your organization.

Be on guard against the halo effect. The *halo effect* happens when the interviewer is swayed by some positively perceived characteristic of the candidate that stands out above all others — for example, the way the candidate looks or dresses, a smooth and well-rehearsed presentation of his or her experience, and so on.

Related to the halo effect is a natural tendency to be guided by personal biases, which leads people to stereotype interview subjects. Each of us has his or her own beliefs and values, and when we think that someone shares our values we tend to be biased toward them. This bias may include age, race, gender, previous work experiences, personal shared experiences, and so on.

As you react to people when you're interviewing them, be constantly alert for the possibility that your personal biases will influence your decision making.

Similarly, any unfavorable information about a candidate may sway the direction of your decision. People generally pay attention to and remember negative experiences more than positive ones. The same mechanism is likely to happen during an interview. Unfavorable information about a candidate may far outweigh numerous favorable bits of information. Don't let that distortion bias your selection decision.

First impressions are powerful influences on the way people assess each other. Be aware of that natural tendency, and make sure you don't allow the first impression an interview subject makes determine how you make a selection decision.

Finally, be on the lookout for what many experts call *cultural noise*. Cultural noise is when an applicant gives you answers that he or she believes you want to hear, rather than answers that express how he or she really feels.

One of the best ways to protect yourself against cultural noise is to avoid leading questions, such as "Do you think that having a long-range vision is a necessary characteristic of a good leader?" Instead, ask open-ended questions, such as, "What do you believe are the necessary characteristics of a good leader?" or "Tell me about some of the problems you've had in other leadership positions and how you dealt with them."

One process you may follow to avoid interviewing errors, is to put the candidate through interviews with several people separately. If you do this, you need to have an objective method, such as a rating scale, for all the interviewers to use to arrive at a group decision.

Some basic training for the individuals who conduct these pre-employment interviews will help the process. Interviewers need to learn how to ask job-related questions, focusing on a candidate's work history, as well as the role of equal employment opportunity issues in the screening process.

Monitoring and adjusting as you go

As you put your succession plan into motion, you need to be open to adjusting the plan every step of the way. Here are some steps you can take to make sure that happens:

- ✔ As you encounter problems in the implementation process, keep a record of problems you encounter and solutions you come up with, including both those that were successful and those that weren't. Make a point of highlighting the successful solutions as possible adjustments you may want to make to future implementations of your succession plan.

- ✔ Meet with your succession-planning team weekly during the implementation process to review progress and discuss situations the team has encountered during the implementation process.

- ✔ As you monitor the implementation of your succession plan, continually think about actions that could be taken in future implementations to make them run more smoothly and more effectively. Describe those actions and propose them to your succession-planning team.

- ✔ If you identify any successful solutions that you think have implications for the way things could be improved in a particular department, contact the relevant managers and discuss it with them.

As with any kind of plan in an organization, carefully monitoring its implementation to see what works and what doesn't work is the only way to improve the plan in the future.

Learning from Your Mistakes

Every time you implement your succession plan, it's an opportunity not only to improve future implementations, but also to beneficially influence other processes within your organization:

- ✔ Share the problem records you created while monitoring the implementation with managers and departments involved in the succession process, such as HR, departments containing key talent, top managers, and the board of directors (if you have one).

- ✔ Solicit their suggestions on how you can improve future implementations of your succession plan.

✔ Design or make available training to people involved in the implementation process. For example, you may train managers on how to interview key talent they plan to hire, or how to work most effectively with the HR people who are responsible for identifying internal and external talent.

Chapter 6

Evaluating the Plan's Implementation

. . . .

. . . .

*N*o matter what kind of organization you have, ultimately, you're providing products or services to a customer. In other words, you're creating customer value.

As an organization, you create customer value not only by providing high-quality products or services, but also by having the right people on staff. Your products and services mean nothing if you don't have the right people in place. People are the drivers of customer value.

The central purpose of designing and implementing a succession plan is to make sure you have the best people in place. Succession planning and the implementation of a succession plan is expensive, so your organization needs a way to evaluate whether it's getting its money's worth. And that's where evaluation comes in.

A succession plan evaluation may be broadly focused on the overall plan or targeted at specific components. But no matter what your focus, your evaluation will move through the same five phases, which I cover in this chapter.

Phase 1: Identifying the Criteria for Measuring Success

To evaluate your succession plan, you need to identify the criteria that you'll use to determine whether it works. First, you need to state the goals of your plan. Then you need to translate those goals into specific outcomes. Finally, you need to develop measures that tell you whether you've been successful in achieving those outcomes.

Stating your plan's goals

Successful succession plans have clear and measurable goals. A *goal* is a specific statement about what you want to accomplish, a description of the results you want to attain in the future.

Goals vary considerably from one organization to the next. Smaller organizations will have less complex succession plans with fewer goals; larger organizations will have more complex succession plans with more goals. The goals of a family business's succession plan will differ from the goals of a corporation's succession plan.

Goals also depend on the reasons you're planning and implementing your succession plan in the first place. Is your plan primarily focused on dealing with unexpected departures? Is it more concerned with covering planned departures, such as retirement? Is it a strategic succession plan, developed to cover key personnel needs based on projected changes in the marketplace?

Any succession plan will have specific goals. Here are some examples of goals that may be included in a succession plan:

- ✔ "I own a family business which has grown during the past five years from a two-person enterprise to an organization employing 54 people. Many of my family members are involved in the business. I would like to retire within a year. My goal is to pick someone who will succeed me who will keep growing my business, without in any way jeopardizing the close relationships existing in my family, their financial future, or the future success of my business."

- ✔ "I am the manager of an IT department. Among my many employees is one key programmer whose creative talent stands out above all the others. I can't imagine how my department will survive without him. My goal is to have an emergency succession team in place who will develop a plan that can enable the team to quickly find a candidate with the right competencies to replace my key programmer in the event something happens to him or that he suddenly and unexpectedly decides to leave for some reason."

✔ "I am a CEO of a manufacturing business. Globalization has changed my business. I used to have two assembly plants, one in Texas and one in Nevada. During the past four years I have rapidly expanded, establishing plants in India, Taiwan, and the Philippines. I have several top managers poised to retire. When my managers actually do retire, I want to be prepared. My goal is to develop a succession plan that will allow me to efficiently replace them with candidates who not only are qualified to manage the business as usual, but also have the kinds of competencies needed to lead a global organization, a plan that will enable me to identify people within my organization who can be developed and promoted as well as people drawn from external recruiting sources or other organizations."

✔ "I am the owner of a successful organization that produces a variety of kitchen utensils. Last year, I decided to change the direction of my organization by offering dramatically new kinds of utensils to my customers. As a result, I spent these last several months totally revising my strategic plan. The new products specified in my new plan involve digital technologies, which means I'll need people with different kinds of competencies than those of my current engineers. Meanwhile, I have two key engineers who are scheduled to retire six months from now. My goal is to have a succession plan that will have an efficient process for identifying successor candidates for the two engineers, candidates who have the kinds of digital technology competencies needed to produce the new products, so I can quickly move my organization in my new strategic direction."

As you can see from these examples, goals are often stated as broad descriptions of what you would like to happen in the future. To evaluate your success in achieving these goals, you need to break the goals down into specific outcomes.

Translating your goals into specific outcomes

Using the four examples of goals described in the preceding section, here's how to break those goals into specific outcomes:

✔ **The family business owner who wants to pick a successor who will keep growing the business without jeopardizing close relationships in the family, their financial futures, or**

the future success of the business: This goal boils down to four specific outcomes:

- The successor will continue to grow the business in the future.
- The hiring of the successor won't jeopardize the close relationships existing in the family.
- The hiring of the successor won't jeopardize the financial future of the family.
- The successor will continue to make the business successful in the future.

✔ **The IT manager who wants to establish an emergency succession team that will enable her to quickly find a candidate with the right competencies to replace her key programmer if he departs:** Reaching this goal calls for the achievement of four specific outcomes:

- An emergency succession team will be formed.
- The team will define the competencies needed by the key programmer's replacement.
- The team will develop an effective process for finding a potential replacement for the key programmer.
- The team will be able to quickly identify and hire a replacement for the key programmer when he departs.

✔ **The CEO who wants to develop a succession plan to efficiently replace departing top managers who are qualified to manage the business as usual and who have the kinds of competencies needed to lead a global organization by both developing people within his organization and selecting candidates from external recruiting sources:** Looking closely at his broadly stated goal, it's clear that he has four specific outcomes in mind:

- The succession plan will be efficient.
- The succession plan will define the competencies needed to manage the business as usual and to lead a global organization.
- People will be identified within the organization who, with some development, could have the potential qualifications to be top managers. They will be provided with the training and coaching needed to make sure they have the qualities and competencies necessary to immediately assume vacated top management positions when they open up.

- People from outside the organization will be identified who have the right qualifications and competencies and are ready to assume top management positions.

✔ **The owner of the utensil company with a new strategic plan whose goal is to have a succession plan to ensure that she has replacements for two key engineers who have the kinds of digital technology competencies needed to produce the new products she has in mind and enable her to quickly move her organization in a new strategic direction:** This goal translates to three specific outcomes:

  - The succession plan will define the technological engineering competencies needed to design and produce the new utensils.

  - Through the plan, readily available engineers with the right competencies will be identified within six months.

  - The new hires will be quickly transitioned into their positions as the key engineers retire.

Breaking down broad goals into specific outcomes will make it easier for you to come up with ways to measure your success.

Developing measures of success

After you've identified the specific outcomes, you need to establish measures of their success. Some of these measures (such as "will be identified within six months") are simple yes or no answers to a question: "Did we make our deadline?" Others may require measures such as ratings of the degree of success.

Phase 2: Determining the Types of Data You Need

After you've determined how you're going to measure your plan's success (see the previous section), you're ready to start collecting some data. But hold on: Before you can start *collecting* data, you need to know what kind of data you're going to collect. There are three main types of data: non-metric, metric, and qualitative. I cover all three in the following sections.

Yes or no: Non-metric data

Non-metric data may sound complicated, but it's just data that's not numerical. In evaluating a succession plan, you usually use non-metric data to determine if you've achieved some overall outcomes for a component of your plan.

You can gather non-metric data by asking yes-or-no questions. Here are some examples:

- ✔ Did you get the support you needed for your succession plan?

- ✔ Did your succession planning team include strategies needed to achieve your goal by establishing a succession plan?

- ✔ Were you able to find a candidate with all the competencies specified in your plan?

- ✔ Did you succeed in transitioning your new hire within the timeframe specified in your plan?

- ✔ Did the transition go smoothly?

- ✔ Were you able to develop and implement your plan without going over budget?

- ✔ Given the time, money, and effort invested in your plan, do you think developing and implementing the plan was cost-effective?

Answering no to such questions generally opens the door to more questions. The answers to those questions then give you information about *why* your plan isn't working, which, in turn, leads you to ideas for changing the plan to make it work more successfully in the future.

You also can generate non-metric data by asking a question that yields several specific answers. For example:

- ✔ In what ways has the succession plan helped you improve the ways in which people are developed in your organization to prepare them as potential successors for vacant key positions?

- ✔ Which talent sources are turning out to be the most useful to you in your search for replacements?

- ✔ In what ways has the internal development of people in the organization as a result of implementing your succession plan affected turnover and retention rates?

- ✔ In what ways has your succession-planning process either raised or lowered employee morale in your organization?

- ✔ In what ways has the hiring processes of the succession plan helped improve the quality of people needed for key positions?

- ✔ As a result of implementing your succession plan, what additional information have you learned about the specific competencies and talents needed in key positions at various levels of your organization?

> ✔ In what ways has the succession plan, through its emphasis on focusing on competency and hiring qualified people, helped you improve processes, productivity, the quality of work, and the creation of customer value?
>
> ✔ In what ways has the succession plan saved you costs through more productive and efficient work?

These kinds of questions yield non-metric data that provides information about the parts of your plan that are working best, which, in turn, will lead you to ideas for altering the plan to make it work even more successful in the future.

Metric data

Metric data is expressed on some kind of numerical scale, such as hours, percentages, ratios, averages, financial costs, and so on. You'll use metric data to evaluate numerous aspects of your succession plan. For example, when you implement your succession plan:

> ✔ How long does it take for your organization to find and hire candidates to replace key employees?
>
> ✔ What percentage of vacancies in key positions are you able to fill?
>
> ✔ How many vacant positions have you filled since your plan was implemented?
>
> ✔ How many people have you identified and developed within your organization in an effort to prepare them to fill vacant positions?
>
> ✔ What is the ratio of the number of people recruited from within your organization to the number of people recruited from external sources?
>
> ✔ How much has your succession plan saved you as a result of more productive and efficient work?

 Metric data is really most useful when you compare it to baseline data (data on how you were doing *before* the plan was implemented). See Chapter 5 for more on collecting baseline data.

Qualitative data

Qualitative data is verbal or narrative in nature. Typically, this type of data is collected by asking *open-ended questions* — questions designed to encourage full, meaningful answers.

Although qualitative data doesn't give you a precise quantification of the success of your plan and its implementation, it does give you very valuable information about the content and processes involved in your plan, which is useful in tweaking the plan to make sure it's the best it can be.

Three ways of gathering qualitative data are particularly useful when evaluating a succession plan: interviews, questionnaires, and focus groups.

Interviews

Conduct interviews with at least a sample of all the participants in the succession plan:

- ✓ **Succession-planning team members:** Get their perceptions of the effectiveness of the development phase of the succession-planning process, as well as suggestions for what could be done differently in the future.

- ✓ **HR personnel:** Find out what kinds of problems and/or successes they experienced when they tried to carry out the plan.

- ✓ **Managers who are directly affected by the succession plan:** Some will be reporting to new top managers, some will be interacting with new colleagues, and some will be dealing with new employees hired to fill vacant key positions. Ask them to describe their experiences with these transitions.

Questionnaires

Include two or three open-ended questions in a questionnaire and distribute it to people in specific groups involved in or affected by the plan. Guarantee their anonymity by asking them not to put their names on the questionnaires and having them deposit them in a centrally located box.

You can target your questionnaires to specific groups of people:

- ✓ **Employees who are now reporting to a new manager as a result of the succession plan:** Ask them to describe what they experienced during the transition from their old manager to their new manager. In what positive or negative ways was their job affected by having a new manager?

- ✓ **HR personnel responsible for carrying out the succession plan:** What kinds of problems did they run into carrying out the tasks and to what extent do they think they succeeded? What suggestions do they have for how the plan could be more easily and effectively undertaken in the future?

✔ **New hires:** Ask new hires to describe their experiences transitioning into their new jobs. What kinds of things made it easy for them? What kinds of things made it difficult? Based on their experiences, what suggestions do they have for improving the transition process in the future?

You can set up an online questionnaire that handles responses anonymously. Sites such as SurveyBuilder (`www.surveybuilder.com`) are a great place to start.

Focus groups

Form focus groups composed of people involved in or affected by specific components of the succession plan. Then facilitate a discussion about their experiences with the succession plan and ask them to give you suggestions for making the plan more effective. For example:

✔ **Form a focus group composed of the people involved in searching for, selecting, and/or developing potential successor candidates.** Facilitate a discussion with them about possible ways they could streamline processes and/or collaborate with one another to get their tasks done more efficiently.

✔ **Form a focus group of employees affected by the plan as a result of reporting to a new manager or working with a new co-worker.** Get them to discuss how their experiences with the new people have in any way affected their feelings about their jobs, the way they perform their jobs, and their thoughts about the organization's future and their roles in it.

✔ **Several months after implementing your succession plan, form a focus group consisting of all the new hires the plan yielded.** Get them to describe their experiences as they transitioned into their new jobs and ask them to tell you what you could have done to make those transitions smoother.

Although qualitative data yields a tremendous amount of valuable information, you need more than qualitative data to effectively assess a succession plan. Qualitative findings provide a broad range of opinions and suggestions, but by their very nature, such findings don't consistently convert into a reliable measure. That's okay, though — you still need qualitative data.

Think of it this way: Metric data tells you whether the plan is meeting your goals. Qualitative data tells you why the plan is (or isn't) meeting your goals and what you can do to improve in the future.

Phase 3: Monitoring Your Plan and Collecting Data

The next step in your evaluation is to establish an ongoing schedule for monitoring your plan and collecting data.

The underlying goal of your evaluation is to determine how effective your succession plan is in achieving its specified outcomes. What those outcomes are and how many of them you list will be a function of the kind of succession plan you've developed. For example, the steps listed in a simple emergency CEO succession plan will involve far fewer outcomes than a broad, strategic succession plan that focuses organization-wide on a variety of people having the kinds of competencies needed to achieve your organizational mission. In other words, the degree of complexity of your evaluation plan and the type and amount of data you collect will be a function of the degree of complexity of your succession plan.

No matter how complex your plan is, one approach is particularly helpful in laying out an evaluation strategy. It's called the six-question approach:

- **Who is responsible for collecting the data needed to evaluate your succession plan?** If you have a large, comprehensive succession plan, you'll probably need several people.

  Use people outside the development team to monitor the plan, if possible. If possible, hire an outside consultant who has no organizational agenda.

- **What specific questions will your data collectors be asking?** Depending on the complexity of your plan, you may have a few simple questions or a large variety of questions aimed at different parts of your succession plan.

- **When will particular questions be asked?** You don't have to wait until the plan has been implemented to evaluate it — your data collectors can start asking questions during the planning process, throughout the plan's implementation, and after the implementation.

- **Where will the questions be asked?** Will the data collectors be interviewing individuals in specific departments? Will they be asking questions in a focus group? Will people be given questionnaires to fill out at their own desks?

- **Why will you be asking the questions you choose to ask?** Will you be looking for a way to measure the success of a given component? Will you be looking for ways to overcome implementation problems? Will you be looking for ways to improve the entire succession-planning process?

✔ **How will the questions be asked?** Will they be asked by a facilitator? Will they be asked by an interviewer? Or will they be asked in a questionnaire?

Following this approach will give you all the questions you need to ask to collect the data required to set up an effective evaluation strategy. Now it's time to set up a schedule for monitoring the plan as it unfolds.

Suppose you're developing and implementing an emergency succession plan for your top executive. You want to be able to identify and hire a qualified replacement in the event that your CEO departs unexpectedly. And you want to accomplish this goal within three months of the departure.

What you're evaluating here is the implementation of a plan you've already created. You can use these same basic steps to evaluate your planning process or to evaluate the succession plan six months after it's implemented.

Start by determining exactly what period of time your evaluation covers. In this case, you're evaluating the implementation process, which (in this example) lasts three months from the time that the departure is announced. Then list your desired outcomes for this timeframe, the kinds of data you'll collect to assess the outcomes, who will be responsible for making it happen, and by when. Here's an example:

✔ Locate people either from within the organization or from outside recruitment sources, who have the competencies needed to assume the executive position. To evaluate this outcome, you need to collect the following data:

- How many qualified potential candidates were you able to identify?

- How many of them were drawn from within your organization and how many from external sources?

- How effective were your search criteria in looking for potential replacements?

✔ If you need to replace the suddenly departing executive with an interim executive, provide the training and support needed to bring that person up to speed. To evaluate this outcome, you need to collect the following data:

- Interview the interim executive to determine whether the training was available, easily provided, and useful.

- Interview appropriate people to determine the degree to which they're willing to support the interim executive.

✔ Find a qualified candidate to assume the executive position on a more permanent basis by March 1. To evaluate this outcome, you need to collect the following data:

- Was the successor found in time?

- To what extent does the successor have the qualifications specified in the succession plan?

You could set up a similar evaluation of the six-month period *after* the implementation of the succession plan is complete. For example:

The transition to a new executive should go smoothly and without any significant problems. To evaluate this outcome, you need to collect the following data:

- Interview the new executive to explore his or her perception of any factors that facilitated or hindered a smooth transition to the new position.

- Interview managers to determine their levels of satisfaction with the executive and how the transition occurred.

- Interview employees to determine their levels of satisfaction with the new executive, as well as their levels of comfort with the way in which he or she is running the organization.

 This is just one example, of course. Your own evaluation will very likely include a variety of other steps and types of data to be collected.

Phase 4: Sifting Through the Data

Depending on the size and scope of your succession plan, you'll collect a range of non-metric, metric, and qualitative data (see "Phase 2: Determining the Types of Data You Need," earlier in this chapter). Your task now is to sort through the data and determine the degree of success of your succession plan. In what ways did the plan work? In what ways did it not work?

 Here are some examples of questions to ask when sifting through the data:

✔ Overall, judging by the data you collected, how successful was the implementation of your succession plan?

✔ How efficiently and effectively did the succession-planning team develop an adequate succession plan?

✔ Did they successfully define the kinds of competencies needed by successors?

✔ What percentages of outcomes did you successfully achieve?

✔ To what extent were you able to locate qualified candidates as successors to potentially vacant positions?

✔ How quickly were you able to complete each of the tasks required to achieve the various outcomes?

✔ How successful were you in achieving a smooth transition in replacing vacant positions?

✔ How favorably were any successions received by your managers?

✔ How favorably were any successions received by your employees?

✔ Looking back at the way your organization functioned before you implemented the succession plan and the way it's functioning now, how worthwhile was the investment of time, money, and effort?

Again, these are just example questions. The specific questions you ask will be a function of the kind of plan you implement and your desired outcomes.

Phase 5: Making Recommendations

During the course of your data collection, you more than likely collected a great deal of qualitative data. That qualitative data is a potential goldmine of recommendations. Not only will it give you suggestions for how to improve your succession-planning process, but it may also point to other improvements you could make in future successions and in your organization itself.

For example, you may discover any or all of the following:

✔ **Your existing job descriptions for key positions are inadequate.** If so, you need to spend time redefining those job descriptions and clarifying the competencies needed to make them successful.

✔ **The leadership styles currently existing in your organization aren't as effective as they could be in inspiring and stimulating employees to perform at top levels.** If so, you need to provide people with leadership training to help them become more effective.

✔ **Your organization has a pool of untapped personnel resources — people who, with the proper training and development, could advance to key positions when needed.** If so, you can put in place training programs to help them develop their skills.

✔ **A larger variety of external recruiting sources is available than you previously realized.** If so, you can tap these resources to fill positions that are open now or will be open in the future.

Qualitative data requires a bit more analysis than numbers or simple yes-or-no responses, but if you take the time to learn from what people tell you, your organization will reap the rewards. Plus, your employees will see that their opinions were taken into consideration.

Chapter 7

Overcoming Obstacles in Implementing Your Plan

. . . .

In This Chapter

▶ Seeing potential obstacles before they crop up

▶ Tackling all kinds of obstacles and moving on

. . . .

Developing and implementing a plan rarely goes as smoothly as you would like. Chances are, you'll run into some obstacles. Some will be simple and easy to overcome. Others will be more complex and more difficult. How prepared you are to deal with obstacles will have a direct impact on the success or failure of your plan.

In this chapter, I give you examples of common obstacles that crop up when implementing a succession plan, suggestions for overcoming these obstacles, and strategies for avoiding them in the first place.

Anticipating Obstacles and Preparing to Deal with Them

The best guard against succession-planning obstacles is to prepare yourself for them in advance. Anticipate the kinds of obstacles you're likely to run into right from the start by doing the following:

> ✔ **If you tried succession planning in the past and it failed, identify the obstacles that prevented it from working (including the people, processes, procedures, or organizational practices).** What actions could you take with your current succession plan to avoid them or at least deal with them if they occur?

✔ **Review any previous experiences you've had developing and implementing other kinds of plans.** Think about any obstacles you ran into during those experiences. What actions did you take to overcome them? If there were any obstacles you weren't able to overcome, how would you handle them differently now?

✔ **Early on in the planning development phase, brainstorm with your succession-planning team members.** Together, based on your collective experiences, try to anticipate the kinds of problems you're likely to encounter in developing and implementing your succession plan and generate ideas for either preventing their occurrence or dealing with them if they do occur.

✔ **Consider potential obstacles internal to your organization.** Are you getting enough support for succession planning? Do you have any managers who are likely to be resistant to a plan? Are there any processes in place in your organization that you think may hinder the implementation of your plan?

✔ **Consider potential obstacles external to your organization.** Are there trends occurring in the marketplace that point to a need for a new style of leadership? Does a review of competitors and customer feedback point to the need for new sets of competencies in key positions?

✔ **Avoid any misunderstandings of your succession plan by clearly and effectively communicating it throughout your organization.**

Anticipating obstacles at the start can save you many headaches down the road. As Winston Churchill said, "Let our advance worrying become advance thinking and planning."

Pushing Past Planning Obstacles

Obstacles will rear their ugly heads even during the development phase of your succession plan. In fact, the occurrence of obstacles during the pre-implementation period gives the succession-planning team a great opportunity to learn how to deal with them. It also gives them helpful practice for dealing with other obstacles that may occur during the implementation phase.

When your planning team doesn't play well together

A potential obstacle during the development phase of your succession planning is not having an effective planning team in place.

When the group fails to function as a smoothly operating team, it can sabotage your entire succession-planning and implementation process. So, you need to select people who are able to collaborate well with one another.

Consider implementing some basic team-building training to help them function effectively as a team.

Here are the core characteristics of successful teams that you're striving for:

✔ **Trust:** Trust is built upon a foundation of safety and confidence. People in a team feel safe when they know they won't be ridiculed, embarrassed, controlled, manipulated, exploited, or punished in any way by other team members.

✔ **Competence and cooperation:** A well-functioning team is an all-competent, cooperative group of individuals, striving to reach goals and levels of excellence that are hard to accomplish with one person alone. Each person brings his or her own areas of expertise to bear on developing an effective plan, while sharing a clear direction. Team members harmonize with one another. They don't waste energy.

✔ **Objectivity:** In a well-functioning team, a climate of objectivity prevails. People value and welcome diverse viewpoints in their efforts to achieve agreed-upon goals.

✔ **Positive attitudes:** A well-functioning team is made up of people whose attitudes are positive, not judgmental. Team members are focused on solving problems and improving things, not on finger pointing and blaming. The best teams are those in which everyone focuses on and acknowledges what others do right, instead of criticizing and disparaging them for what they do wrong.

The more effectively your planning team truly works as a team, the higher the probability of your ending up with a well-developed succession plan and strategies for overcoming any implementation obstacles that may occur.

When your succession plan conflicts with your overall strategic plan

One of the most damaging obstacles to the entire development of a succession plan and implementation process is not having the succession plan anchored to your organization's strategic plan. All the time and effort you and your team spend developing a carefully constructed succession plan will do you no good in the long run if it isn't anchored to your organization's strategic plan.

Review and discuss your organization's strategic plan with your planning team right at the beginning of the plan development process. Make sure everybody thoroughly understands and supports it. New hires will have an easier time transitioning into your organization if their values are in sync with your organization's core values. So, all team members need to be onboard with the strategic plan and use it to guide their decision making as they work on your succession plan.

Here are two considerations to keep in mind as you review and discuss your strategic plan:

✔ **A central focal point of any strategic plan is your organization's long-range vision, what you want your organization to be in the future.** All the succession-planning team members must share a clear picture of this organizational vision, and anybody you hire should understand and agree that a key part of his or her role is to help your organization work toward that vision.

✔ **An organization's core values and long-range vision are usually translated into a clear mission statement.** Again, the succession-planning team members must be aware of and fully understand the organizational mission. That understanding will play a key role in the succession decisions that they make.

If you fail to ensure that your succession plan is anchored to your strategic plan, you run the risk of making many inappropriate decisions as you try to implement your plan.

When you don't have a supportive planning environment

Another potential obstacle during the development phase is not having a supportive planning environment. A supportive environment is one in which all the team members are able to commit fully to the succession-planning process, the room you're working in is comfortable, you have enough time to do the work, and the meeting is well organized.

In the following sections, I offer tips on how to address any issues that are preventing you from having a supportive environment.

If members of the planning team are preoccupied with their regular responsibilities

All succession-planning team members must see succession planning as a high priority for the organization and know that their participation is seen as a highly valuable contribution to the organization.

If it seems like team members aren't focusing on their work on the planning team, see if you can figure out why. Are they stressed by their other responsibilities? If so, maybe you can talk to their managers about getting some extra help to cover for them during the planning process. Maybe it's just a matter of the team members asking for the help they need.

Team members must be given additional assistance in their departments so they can feel confident that important tasks are still getting done in their absence. This will help them feel less stressed as they participate in the planning process.

If the physical setting for the planning meetings isn't comfortable

Provide the team with a comfortable meeting room, preferably away from the organization (instead of a regular conference room within the organization, with all the distracting activities that usually take place around it). This simple step will reinforce the importance of what they're doing.

Provide the team with every tool or piece of equipment they need to work efficiently with one another, such as flip charts, an overhead projector, snacks, and so on.

If not enough time is allotted for the planning meetings

When setting up any planning session, allow enough time for each participant to be able to walk away feeling that he or she has made some progress in developing the plan.

If finalizing a succession plan is urgent, you may want to hold planning meetings once a week for two or three hours (but not more than half a day). If there is no critical urgency for completing the succession plan, another alternative is to hold the meetings once a month for a full day or two in a retreat-type session.

If the structure of the meetings isn't well organized

Hire a facilitator to run the meetings, preferably someone who isn't part of your organization and has the objectivity and skills needed to ensure that the sessions run smoothly. With the help of the facilitator, make sure there is a clear and detailed agenda for every session.

Near the end of each meeting, as the planning process progresses, specify tasks that need to be completed or information that needs to be gathered in preparation for the subsequent meeting, and assign specific responsibilities to each team member.

Jumping the Obstacles People Put Up

Once you've developed your succession plan and begun implementing it, you may find yourself running into a number of obstacles that have to do with how people are feeling or reacting to the implementation. In this section, I cover the various people who may be less than helpful along the way.

When your CEO is the problem

It should come as no surprise that the CEO plays a major role in the success of your succession plan. Given the power and span of control exercised by the CEO, the lack of that person's support for succession planning can be a very difficult obstacle to overcome, especially if the CEO's successor is the one being considered.

Here are some obstacles that a CEO may pose:

- ✔ The CEO may assume that succession planning is too complicated, too distracting in the face of the everyday work that needs to be done, too time consuming, and costs too much to make it worthwhile.

- ✔ If your CEO is also the founder of your organization, or if the CEO has transformed it from a small, struggling business to a large, successful company, the CEO may find it very difficult to leave and subconsciously block any attempts to find his or her successor.

- ✔ Your CEO may have — how can I put this delicately? — an exaggerated sense of his or her own importance. It's natural — the CEO is at the helm of a complex organization, overseeing many people and many functions, and making many critical decisions. But when the CEO thinks he or she can't be replaced, you have an obstacle on your hands.

- ✔ Your CEO may define himself or herself in terms of the job. Giving up that job is emotionally difficult. As a result, the CEO may be reluctant to let go.

- ✔ The CEO may fear that succession planning will start a competition among other top managers in the company for that top position, and worry that the managers won't be able to collaborate productively as a management team.

- ✔ The CEO may strongly favor as a successor a particular top manager from within the organization — someone with whom he or she has developed a close and loyal relationship. The

CEO may push that person above other potentially more qualified candidates.

✔ If your organization has a board of directors, they may be reluctant to let the CEO go, because the CEO has been so instrumental in making the organization successful.

So, how do you overcome such CEO-related obstacles?

✔ **Engage everyone — from the CEO to the board to the managers and employees — in long-term thinking by discussing the succession plan in the context of your organization's strategic plan.** Emphasizing the critical importance of the succession plan to the future of the organization will help people set aside their fears.

✔ **If your CEO is having difficulty letting go of the job, hire a coach to help him or her through the process.** Retiring isn't a cakewalk, and there are consultants who specialize in helping people make that transition.

✔ **Hire an external consultant to facilitate the entire succession-planning and development process.** You want someone who can think long-term and help the planning team work quickly and effectively. Ideally, that person also will have the skills to coach the CEO (see the preceding bullet).

✔ **If you have a board of directors that's supportive of succession planning, enlist their help in getting the CEO to think long term and/or deal with his or her feelings about being succeeded by someone else.**

When other people are standing in your way

The CEO isn't the only one who may unintentionally (or not so unintentionally) stand in the way of your succession plan's success:

✔ **Some employees, busily completing their everyday tasks, may not support succession planning because they see it as just another time-wasting bureaucratic process piled on top of other bureaucratic processes.** As a result, when called upon to make a contribution to some aspect of the succession plan, they drag their feet, doing as little as they can get away with, which slows the plan's implementation, hindering its effectiveness.

✔ **Some people — particularly those who don't feel secure in their jobs — may see having to report to a new manager as a threat.** They may be afraid that they'll lose their jobs because the new managers, with their new management styles, will disapprove of the way they do things. Because of these worries, they'll give little or no support to the succession plan.

✔ **Over time, people get used to doing their jobs a certain way, which intensifies their resistance to change.** They may see succession planning as a threat because new people will force them to do things in a different way.

✔ **People may withhold support for a succession plan because they don't really understand it.** Not knowing what the plan is all about may lead to the spreading of false rumors, such as: "They're thinking about eliminating positions."

✔ **If your succession plan is narrowly defined, some people may feel left out and not support it.** They see it as a plan directed only at covering people who occupy senior-level positions.

✔ **People may be envious of their co-workers' success.** Succession planning generally includes developing and promoting people from within the organization. When some people see that happening to others, but not to themselves, they may worry about losing their own jobs (or just be blinded by envy).

✔ **When it comes to promoting people into positions that need to be covered, managers often lean toward supporting their "favorites," in spite of the fact that there may be other employees who are even more qualified.** The morale and, hence, the performance of those other people suffers when they see that happening.

✔ **Some people in key positions may feel very threatened when they see other people being developed to take their place.** An important component of a comprehensive succession plan is taking steps to make sure that candidates are available to cover key positions important to the organization's success, if those positions are unexpectedly vacated.

Although there are no easy solutions to these obstacles, here are two things you can do to reduce the likelihood of their occurring:

✔ **Clearly and thoroughly communicate, throughout your organization, what the succession plan is all about.** Communication will go a long way toward overcoming people obstacles. With the very visible support of the CEO (and board of directors, if you have one), the plan should be published and distributed to everyone and discussed in meetings at every level.

✔ **Make sure that every manager is fully informed on all aspects of the succession plan.** In discussing the succession plan in department meetings, managers must be prepared to answer any questions related to the plan. In fact, a good practice is for managers to solicit questions about concerns anyone may have about the succession plan, with ready answers to help eliminate fears, confusion, and misinformation.

More than ever in today's media-connected work environment, open communication is very important. The more people know about where the organization is going and what's happening, the less susceptible they'll be to distracting rumors that often impede performance.

When skepticism reigns

There is one set of people obstacles that deserves special attention: employees who are unwilling to support the implementation of any succession plan because they're skeptical. These folks are the ones who say things like, "It's been tried before and it failed! All it did was cause us a lot of work that went nowhere. What a waste of time!"

Again, communication is a strategy for overcoming this obstacle:

- ✔ Acknowledge the past failure, explain why it didn't work in the past, and clearly articulate what will be done differently this time around to make sure the plan works.

- ✔ Solicit ideas from employees on steps you could take to make sure the plan works. This will give employees a sense of ownership of the plan, strengthening their support of it.

Solving Process Problems

Another set of potential obstacles has to do with the implementation process itself, as your succession plan is rolled out, step-by-step. These process obstacles fall into three categories: time, design, and accountability.

Time

Time is a big factor in everything we do. People complain about the lack of time and about how much time it takes to get something done. Attitudes toward how time is used can create significant obstacles to the implementation of succession plans.

For example, when the succession-planning team completed its plan, team members probably were satisfied with the time schedule they constructed for the completion of the various tasks in the plan. During implementation, however, it may become apparent that the schedule is a superficial one at best. People may be confused by a lack of clarity or detail in the sequence of target times for the completion of tasks.

Although succession-planning team members may have thought that the target times were realistic, it may turn out that the target times are unrealistic, either not allowing enough time or allowing too much time.

Typically, people and organizations have a lot to do. Time is valuable. When assigned succession tasks need to be completed, some employees try to find ways to carry them out as quickly as possible, so they can get back to their regular jobs. Unfortunately, moving too quickly could result in making poor decisions. More often than not, finding, selecting, and hiring qualified people takes time.

Here are ways you can overcome time-related obstacles:

- ✓ **The best way to avoid time obstacles is to make them an important topic of discussion during the succession-planning process.** When specifying target times for particular tasks, go to the people who will be responsible for carrying them out. Interview them to make sure that what you're setting up is realistic.

- ✓ **Be sure to monitor and guide the implementation process.** Assign one or more key individuals to actively track the progress of the implementation process and take appropriate steps to keep it moving in line with the established time frame and deadlines. You may want to assign or hire additional resources to help people who are responsible for meeting a particular time target.

- ✓ **If you encounter time-related obstacles, be flexible and adjust your target times if necessary.**

Design

Your succession-planning team worked hard to design an action plan. And when they complete the plan, they leave that comfortable conference room satisfied that the plan can be smoothly implemented. However, they sometimes find themselves running into obstacles during its implementation because some aspects of the plan's design don't fit the "real world." For example:

- ✓ During implementation, you may realize that some of the steps described in the plan weren't detailed enough. As a result, time targets are missed because new processes need to be developed.

- ✓ On the opposite end of the spectrum, some steps outlined in the plan may turn out to be too complicated, too time-consuming, or too burdensome to be effectively carried out. Again, as a result, time is lost as new, streamlined processes have to be developed.

✔ Some steps in the plan may require too much documentation. Busy people in most organizations have a low tolerance for filling out forms or reports. Already overburdened with the responsibilities of their own jobs, they don't place a high priority on implementation paperwork. As a result, necessary documentation may end up being overlooked.

✔ There may be no mechanism for ongoing communication of the plan and its progress. This situation could lead to confusion or misunderstanding about the plan, which may even result in talented people, who think the plan won't help them, deciding to leave.

Here are some suggestions for overcoming these obstacles:

✔ **The best way to avoid design obstacles is to engage the help of the people who will be responsible for carrying out the plan during the plan development phase.**

✔ **Make sure your succession-planning team members are available to quickly react.** You can help them do this by getting them to streamline processes that aren't working and minimize documentation requirements wherever they can.

✔ **Publish a succession-plan newsletter.** This newsletter could be a brief two- to four-page document that comes out periodically during the implementation phase, describing tasks being undertaken; progress being made; and people being hired, promoted, or moved to new positions. It also could describe obstacles encountered and invite readers to send in ideas for overcoming them, which would give everyone a sense of participation in the implementation and reinforce a problem-solving mindset among employees in your organization.

Accountability

No matter how clear and detailed your succession plan may be, you'll invariably run into instances where something fails to get done. The key issue in such situations is that someone must be accountable. Here are some accountability obstacles that may occur:

✔ **Tasks specified in the plan don't get completed effectively, exactly as planned, or on time.** This happens when there isn't adequate supervision by succession-planning team members because they're too busy working hard at fulfilling their other job responsibilities.

✔ **Team members responsible for the implementation of particular steps in the succession plan have difficulty overcoming the consequences of turf protection.** For example, some managers or supervisors may view the hiring of particular candidates as a threat to their own departments. As a result, they end up wanting to reject qualified candidates. Team members are responsible for making sure this doesn't happen.

✔ **People who busily carry out their primary responsibilities tend to procrastinate on assignments that they regard as less significant, such as implementing particular steps of the succession plan.**

Here are some suggestions for overcoming these obstacles:

✔ Primary accountability for the success of the succession plan rests with the members of the succession-planning team, because they're the ones most intimately familiar with your plan. They need to give their succession-related responsibilities the highest priority, no matter what their regular positions demand of them.

✔ Team members need to be constantly monitoring the implementation. Like an emergency-response team, they need to make themselves available to step in whenever something isn't proceeding properly and find ways of adjusting what's happening to make it work.

✔ Succession-planning team members must be constantly alert to people procrastinating and be ready to step in and prod them to complete their portion of the implementation plan.

Staying on Task

Another set of potential obstacles has to do with the specific tasks that need to be completed as your succession plan is rolled out. These task obstacles fall into five categories: analysis, recruitment, people development, selection, and hiring.

When you're having trouble with analysis

When you're looking to hire someone at any level, you have to identify the knowledge, skills, competencies, and talents needed to perform that job. This calls for job analysis. Several obstacles can get in the way:

✔ **Your organization may not have an adequate process for systematically determining the competencies needed to perform a particular job.** This is a critical obstacle when searching for a successor to a key position. How can you find a qualified candidate when you don't know exactly what you're looking for?

✔ **Your organization may not have an effective performance appraisal system.** Only by constantly being in touch with how well people are doing, the kinds of problems they're running into, and what needs to be done to help them perform more effectively will you really be able to identify the qualities you're looking for in a replacement.

✔ **Particularly in large organizations with many business units and a complex mission, the people charged with the responsibility of finding successor candidates may not be totally aware of critical factors occurring in the marketplace, such as changing customer needs and the emergence of powerful competitors.** These factors may very likely reshape their notion of the kinds of people needed to fill vacant positions.

✔ **The people charged with the responsibility of finding successor candidates may not be totally aware of or have a system for identifying future competencies needed to implement the organization's strategic plan and move the organization closer to its objectives.**

To avoid these obstacles, your organization must have a well thought-out system for analyzing jobs, appraising performance, and determining needed job competencies. In today's rapidly changing, technologically sophisticated world, the competencies needed for jobs are constantly changing. Without such a job-analysis system, you'll be left behind.

When you're not finding the right people for the job

After you've defined the competencies needed by a successor to fill your vacant position, one of the first things you consider doing is recruiting people through sources external to your organization. But several obstacles can get in the way:

✔ **You may have an ineffective recruitment strategy.** The strategy may not be articulated clearly enough. It may be too complex and cumbersome. It may not be flexible enough in the face of constantly changing market conditions.

✔ **You may have an inadequate data pool of previous candidates you considered for positions, or you may lack the search tools to find people in this pool.** A job candidate who may have been your second choice for a given position may still be available if the position now becomes vacant. And given changes that take place in job requirements due to changing markets, competition, or new directions in your strategic plan, you may find other people who now fill the bill.

✔ **You may be understaffed or faced with an unusually urgent need to find a replacement.** Reading résumés, checking references, and interviewing and screening candidates take time.

✔ **Depending on the degree of specialization of your product or service, you may find an inadequate supply of external candidates for your needs.** This situation is especially likely in today's global marketplace, in which people are increasingly mobile in their search for other opportunities.

✔ **Even if you find an interested candidate, you may discover that you aren't able to offer salary and benefits that are competitive in your marketplace.**

Here are some suggestions for avoiding or overcoming such obstacles:

✔ Develop a comprehensive recruitment strategy. Make sure each step is clearly defined and not too complicated or time-consuming.

✔ Make more use of the Internet. Post your position on professional association websites, vendor websites, in the classified sections of newspaper websites, and, of course, on your own website. (If you haven't already established an online presence, do it now.)

✔ Because some candidates post their résumés on various employment sites, visit these sites regularly and use key words to search their résumé databases.

✔ Implement an internal referral program in which employees who refer candidates who are hired and stay on the job for at least three months are given a cash bonus or other incentive.

✔ Expand your contacts with executive search firms, employment agencies, and colleges and universities.

✔ If your organization is part of any trade groups or associations, such memberships can provide valuable networking opportunities and potential sources for candidates. Keep your contacts very much alive with people in these groups.

✔ Keep track of and in contact with individuals you've interviewed in the past who were viable candidates, but not your first choice at the time.

✔ Increase the visibility of your organization by writing interesting articles for trade publications or business sections in newspapers. That kind of visibility helps generate interest from potential candidates.

When developing people within your organization isn't a cakewalk

People within your organization can end up being the perfect candidates for job openings. But several issues can get in the way, such as the following:

✓ **Many people in your organization may be looking for opportunities to advance their careers, but you may be totally unaware of their aspirations.** Without a way to find out who's looking to move up, you run the risk that such employees will leave for jobs elsewhere.

✓ **Your organization may rush to promote people who appear to be qualified, without truly understanding their aspirations and goals.** Some people may accept the new position for a better salary but end up being unhappy because it isn't exactly the direction they wanted to go.

✓ **Inadequate or inaccurate performance appraisals of seemingly promotable employees may end up causing problems in the future.** The existing appraisals may mislead you, or some critical information about the individual may be missing.

✓ **Even if you identify internal candidates you think can be developed as potential replacements for other positions, you may fail to provide them with the kinds of training they need.**

To minimize the possibility of running into these obstacles, take steps to ensure that you have a powerful internal development system in place, a system that helps you identify and capitalize on the aspirations of your employees:

✓ Encourage and even incentivize your managers and supervisors to spend time with and learn about their individual employees.

✓ Improve your performance appraisal system so that it gives you the depth of information you need to evaluate the potential of any employee.

✓ Actively and publicly identify employees who have the potential to move into needed positions and provide them with ample and appropriate training, coaching, and mentoring.

✓ Consider using a resources system to gather, maintain, and update information regarding your employees' experience, training, and expertise. This type of information can help you easily and accurately look at your current employees and determine if there are potential matches between their skill mix and the skills that are required in an open position.

The upside of looking inside your organization for succession candidates is the positive effect it can have on your organizational climate and culture. When people know they have a chance to advance their careers without leaving your organization, they work harder to achieve it. Your retention levels will increase, along with a corresponding decrease in the expenses you would incur recruiting, hiring, orienting, and training new people from the outside.

When you can't make up your mind

You've identified potential candidates and you're ready to select one as the successor. Alas, you may face even more obstacles:

- With all the technological advances, diversity, and mixtures of generations in today's world, applications will reach your desk in a number of different of formats — snail mail, faxes, e-mail, a variety of résumés and forms created by employment agencies. Working though this diversity of submissions takes times.

- If you're in a time of economic downturn, you may receive more applications than you're used to. As a result, you'll find yourself spending a lot of time screening and reviewing résumés, as well as interviewing candidates.

- Many people, who have gone through numerous job interviews, have become very skilled at telling you convincingly what they think you want to hear or what they want you to know about them. You may make the wrong selection, because you ended up evaluating the candidate in a more positive way than you should have.

- In interacting with a candidate, you may make an unconsciously biased decision because you see him or her as very similar to you or very similar to someone you admire. As a result, you may hire the wrong person.

Here are some suggestions that will help you make the best selection:

- Given that a good selection is very important, realize that it will take time. Allow yourself that time. Plan for it. Be patient.

- Involve other people in the selection process of the same candidate so you get different perspectives on the person's qualifications and then make a consensual decision. This strategy will help prevent your own bias from getting in the way.

✔ As you read résumés and conduct job interviews, keep the job specifications clearly in mind as you try to answer two key questions:

- Can the individual do the job? Does he or she have the knowledge, skills, abilities, and training to carry out the job?

- Will the individual do the job? Does his or her work history demonstrate the levels of drive, persistence, energy, initiative, and leadership that are required in the position?

When you've found the right person but hiring hurts

Finally, you've selected a candidate. You still may be faced with a few obstacles:

✔ In spite of the right qualifications, given the idiosyncrasies of any organization, the designated replacement may not be to ready to take over. In your hurry to make sure the position was filled, you may not have given the new person a good enough introduction to your organization. You may not have an adequate process for transferring critical knowledge from the person who previous occupied the position. Or there may have been a general lack of support for the successor as he or she transitioned into the position.

✔ Every organization has its own culture. In spite of your careful interview and selection of the candidate, you may end up with a candidate who doesn't fit into your organizational culture.

Be sure to provide new hires with a thorough orientation to your organization. Make sure they're fully supported on every level as they transition into their new positions.

Part III
Diving Deeper into Succession Planning

The 5th Wave   By Rich Tennant

In this part . . .

When it comes to succession planning, there is no such thing as "one size fits all." The most effective strategic plans are tailored to individual organizations. Organizations are unique, and this uniqueness must be reflected in each succession plan. If your plan isn't custom-made for your organization, it'll be doomed to fail. In this part, you see the importance of making a customized plan for your organization, as well as separate customized plans for each organizational level. This includes a succession plan at the CEO level, as well as plans for your professional positions, technical positions, and other key roles.

This part also shows you how to identify potential job openings, competency requirements, and viable candidates to fill these openings. This part answers the questions: "Who will fit these positions?" and "How do you develop the needed talent?"

Finally, one central goal for any successful succession plan is to implement a smooth and effective transition, and this part provides you with the strategies to do so.

Chapter 8

Covering Key Positions in Your Succession Plan

*Y*our organization's success is built on the contributions of every employee at every level. Employees are your organization's most important resource and valuable asset.

However, in any organization, some employees occupy more critical positions than others, called *key positions*. These positions are key because the people occupying them have the knowledge, experience, and competencies that are especially critical to the success of your organization.

At any time, any one of the people occupying a key position may depart. No matter what the reason for the departures, you need an active process in place for each key position in your succession plan. You can't afford to be without them.

In this chapter, I describe some example considerations for the most important key positions typical of most organizations. Depending on the size and nature of your organization, your key positions may be different and/or be differently titled.

Keep in mind that the goal of this chapter is to provide you with useful examples that you can use as models for tailoring your succession plan to fit your particular needs.

Leadership Positions: Where You Lead, I Will Follow

A person who occupies a leadership position is someone who is able to influence others to come together to accomplish an objective, and provides them with direction, coaching, and support throughout the process. Depending on the size and nature of your organization, leaders are evident at many levels, from the head of the organization to top management to department heads and supervisors.

Note: Every organization has a leader at the top. This leadership position goes by many names, depending on the kind of organization. Chief executive officer (CEO), president, general manager, mayor, senior partner, county administrator, and school superintendent are just a few examples. For convenience in the following discussion, I use the title CEO to refer to the top leader.

CEOs

Of all the key leadership positions, the CEO usually gets the most attention in succession planning, particularly in large organizations.

Why CEOs matter

The CEO occupies a position of central importance in any organization. Here's why:

- ✔ **CEOs are responsible for just about everything.** They're seen by people both within and outside the organization as the person most responsible for its success or failure.

- ✔ **CEOs provide the vision and set the direction of an organization.** They determine which products or services it will provide in which market segment.

- ✔ **CEOs establish and propagate the values of the organization by their behaviors, actions, and decisions.**

- ✔ **CEOs, by exercising their particular styles of leadership, establish the foundation for the creation of the organizational culture.**

- ✔ **CEOs are the ultimate deciders of who occupies other key positions in the organization.**

- ✔ **CEOs are the primary architects of an organization's long-range strategic plan.**

What to look for in a CEO

Your organization's needs in a CEO will depend on the type of organization you have and the particular traits required for the job. But no matter what type of organization you have, the CEO should

- ✔ Look at the organization as an overall system — as an integrated network of people, processes, activities, and technologies, all focused on providing the highest-quality products or services to customers in a competitive marketplace

- ✔ Keep a constant eye on the future, excelling at strategic planning and goal setting and driven by a vision of how the organization can be even more successful

- ✔ Be sensitive to and recognize his or her profound influence on the organizational culture and have the skills to shape that culture along a productive and successful path

- ✔ Have impressive communication skills, especially to articulate his or her vision of the organization to people at every level in the organization, as well as to customers, vendors, and competitors in the marketplace

- ✔ Excel at bringing people together, to work collaboratively with one another as an organization-wide team in the pursuit of a common purpose

- ✔ Be able to inspire and motivate people, focusing and energizing them to achieve the best performance possible as they work toward achieving the organizational mission

- ✔ Have integrity and serve as an example to everyone in the organization by upholding high ethical standards in business practices and individual behavior

- ✔ Have an excellent capacity to analyze large amounts of information, sifting through it with intuitive skills to see new opportunities, and arrive at solid, workable decisions designed to improve the organization's future

- ✔ Be able to recognize talent in others, recognize and develop potential talent, and create a competency-based outlook throughout the organization

- ✔ Have the skills to build an effective top management team

- ✔ Be flexible and able to adapt to and convert unexpected changes to the organization's advantage

- ✔ Be knowledgeable about trends and practices in the marketplace and regulatory policies that affect the organization

In addition to these generic attributes, CEOs may need to have other talents, skills, and competencies in special kinds of organizations, such as foundations or professional associations. For example, the CEO of a foundation needs to be very good at fundraising. The CEO of a professional association needs to be good at designing strategies for increasing association membership. For tips on how to determine these additional attributes, see Chapter 9.

Top management

A variety of titles are used to refer to members of the top management team, each with his or her own set of skills and competencies. In this section, I cover the titles used most frequently in corporations.

Chief operating officer

The chief operating officer (COO) is the person who has a more day-to-day, hands-on responsibility for the way the company operates. His or her goal is to make sure the organization functions smoothly and productively and that everything gets completed on time and at high quality levels.

When you're customizing your succession plan to include COO successors, keep in mind that the ideal COO should

- ✔ Be systems minded and have a process-improvement orientation, encouraging people throughout the organization to constantly improve processes wherever they see more effective or efficient ways of getting things done.

- ✔ Have a problem-solving mindset and the ability to discourage finger pointing among employees and departments when mistakes are made.

- ✔ Be focused on creating customer value based on knowledge of company products, services, and processes, as well as a clear understanding of customer preferences and needs.

- ✔ Have solid business sense and the ability to find new ways to keep operations cost-effective, without sacrificing quality, morale, or customer service.

Chief financial officer

The responsibility of the chief financial officer (CFO) is to manage money and organizational assets and deal with budgets, banks, lenders, and investors.

When you're customizing your succession plan to include CFO successors, keep in mind that the ideal CFO should

- ✔ Be knowledgeable about strategic planning and change management, because an important part of his or her responsibility is to ensure the organization's financial future

- ✔ Be skilled at organizing, developing, and implementing financial plans, because he or she is responsible for overall organizational budget planning and departmental budgets

- ✔ Excel at and be comfortable with detail and accuracy, two important components of financial planning

- ✔ Be good at both oral and written communication, because he or she has to interact with people throughout the organization

- ✔ Be familiar with and up-to-date on any relevant financial and accounting statutes, regulations, and policies of local, state, and federal governments

- ✔ Be flexible and open to change in the face of ever-changing marketplace trends and business conditions

Chief information officer

The chief information officer (CIO) is in charge of an organization's information technology. This means more than just computers and the Internet. The CIO is the organization's chief knowledge officer; he or she establishes the organization's vision from the technology standpoint and leads the implementation of all the organization's technology initiatives.

When you're customizing your succession plan to include CIO successors, keep in mind that the ideal CIO should

- ✔ Have an up-to-date, comprehensive understanding of the newest technology concepts, programs, applications, and principles and their implications for organizational best practices

- ✔ Be able to look across the organization and identify operations, processes, and procedures that lend themselves to newer and more effective high-tech solutions

- ✔ Be effective at collaboration, given the broad reach of information technology throughout the organization and the subsequent need to deal with people at every level

- ✔ Be a creative problem-solver, with the ability to look beyond the obvious and provide IT solutions to a broad range of organizational issues and problems

- ✔ Be able to communicate the value of innovation and adaptation to change, given the pace of advancements in information technology in the 21st-century marketplace

- ✔ Have the financial management skills to balance the costs of acquiring new information technologies with the benefits of more efficient processes and/or increased revenues

✔ Have the leadership ability to form an effective IT team capable of providing IT services throughout the organization and quickly dealing with IT issues (such as inconvenient power outages or program malfunctions) when they occur

Chief marketing officer

The chief marketing officer (CMO) is responsible for the day-to-day marketing operation of an organization — coordinating promotions, advertising, and public relations to increase sales and revenues.

When you're customizing your succession plan to include CMO successors, keep in mind that the ideal CMO should

✔ Be highly creative and able to harness that creativity in helping your organization achieve maximum success in the marketplace

✔ Be able to inspire, stimulate, and nurture marketing creativity in others, particularly members of his or her team

✔ Have solid experience and expertise in all areas related to marketing, such as advertising, online promotions, and new product development and introduction (or at least the ability to rapidly learn the fundamentals of those areas)

✔ Be flexible and have the skill to quickly adjust and update marketing strategies, such as by incorporating social media into the marketing process

✔ Have the business savvy to establish and adhere to marketing budgets, with solid monitoring and controls over expenditures related to advertising campaigns, promotions, and contracts with vendors

Key managers

The leadership positions described in the preceding section are generally thought of as top leadership positions in an organization. However, depending on the size and nature of your organization, numerous other leadership positions may be key to your organization's success. For example, if you're working in an educational organization, you may be focused on finding a successor for the principal. If you're working in a hospital, you may be focused on finding a successor for the director of nursing.

Regardless of the management level or types of managers in your organization, all managers are responsible for the performance of the people reporting to them. This responsibility calls for a common set of managerial attributes and behaviors, all of which must be taken into account when you customize your succession plan.

The ideal manager does the following:

✔ Leads his or her team by working with them to establish goals and the strategies to meet those goals

✔ Motivates and guides employees toward accomplishing specific goals, and provides the members of his or her team with coaching, feedback, and support along the way

✔ Leads meetings and makes responsible decisions, taking employee input into account

✔ Gives constructive performance feedback to employees and helps them identify areas in need of further development and improvement

✔ Is a dedicated coach and mentor who emphasizes to employees that every mistake they make is an opportunity to learn and improve themselves and their work

✔ Arranges for appropriate assignments and training experiences to give employees opportunities to develop themselves

✔ Encourages a spirit of cooperation and an openness to diverse viewpoints and opinions, and discourages finger pointing and blaming

✔ Fosters a climate of mutual trust among employees and encourages them to help each other when needed, even if doing so isn't in their job description

✔ Brings interpersonal conflict into the open, facilitates constructive conflict resolution, and creates win-win-win situations

✔ Has a strategic business sense and an awareness of the organizational impact of business issues, processes, and outcomes

✔ Understands basic business fundamentals, including how his or her own job fits into creating customer value and increasing the bottom line

✔ Understands the business implications of his or her decisions and the actions that result from them

✔ Keeps current with the latest information and best practices in both his or her own field of expertise and the field of management

✔ Is not only open to feedback, but actively seeks it from others in order to determine where further development is needed

✔ Engages in activities such as reading and attending seminars to improve knowledge, abilities, and professional skills as a manager

In the following sections, I cover the key types of managers you may have in your organization.

Human resources manager

The HR manager is responsible for managing organizational personnel needs and developing and training people throughout an organization. In terms of succession planning, the HR manager is a key player involved in defining the needed competencies of successors for any position in the organization, finding potential replacements, screening résumés and applications, interviewing, and formally hiring the selected choices.

When you're customizing your succession plan to include HR manager successors, keep in mind that the ideal HR manager

- ✔ Must be aware of local, state, and federal employment guidelines

- ✔ Should be very organized in terms of storing and accessing employee information, time management, and benefits administration, and should have expertise in the latest human resources systems

- ✔ Should be ethically driven and ensure that the organization's ethical guidelines and standards are followed throughout the organization

- ✔ Should be capable of looking at the needs of people in an organization from both management and employee perspectives and balancing the needs of both

- ✔ Must value fairness and ensure that everyone's voice is heard

- ✔ Must have the skills to be an advocate for employee concerns, while at the same time enforcing management policies

- ✔ Should be able to multi-task, given the challenge of recruiting, dealing with employee issues, interviewing, and numerous other personnel issues

Training manager

The training manager develops, conducts, and implements educational programs for employees, as well as monitors training consultants and external sources of employee training.

When you're customizing your succession plan to include training manager successors, keep in mind that the ideal training manager should

- ✔ Have a broad range of training expertise, not only in terms of training processes and programs, but also in terms of running a training department

✔ Be familiar with the latest theories and insights about how adults learn and know how to design and organize training to deal with different learning styles

✔ Have an up-to-date understanding of available media technology and the role it plays in training

✔ Be well organized and able to quickly develop effective training programs

✔ Be able to develop trainers to conduct future sessions

✔ Be familiar with professional external training sources, suppliers, and contacts

✔ Be a skilled communicator who presents his or her ideas clearly, credibly, and with authority, while simultaneously listening with empathy and building rapport

✔ Be perceptive, flexible, and innovative in order to adjust approaches or modify techniques in training sessions that don't seem to be working as planned

✔ Be skilled at assessment of training effectiveness

Customer service manager

Customer service managers are responsible for overseeing customer service representatives, making sure that all customer questions have been answered and problems quickly and effectively resolved, ascertaining that all orders are processed promptly and accurately, and keeping top management informed about any customer problems.

When you're customizing your succession plan to include customer service manager successors, keep in mind that the ideal customer service manager should

✔ Have strong communication and interpersonal skills, and be able to listen attentively to others, understand customer concerns, and respond in a clear and understanding manner

✔ See the world through a problem-solving lens and strive continuously to effectively resolve customer issues

✔ Be able to develop a collaborative, responsive, and highly motivated team of customer representatives and be able to coach them in solving customer problems

✔ Be able to provide constructive guidance to employees experiencing difficulties with customers, attentively helping them find the best possible resolutions for the organization and the customers

✔ Have strong computer skills and an ability to multi-task

✔ Be capable of working well under stress

✔ Be skilled at conflict resolution and mediation strategies for dealing with angry customers

✔ Be able to process and analyze customer feedback and apply the best suggestions for product or service improvement and resolution of customer problems

Office manager

Office managers are responsible for planning and coordinating office operations and clerical support functions of the organization, as well as managing, storing, and retrieving office records.

When you're customizing your succession plan to include office manager successors, keep in mind that the ideal office manager should

✔ Have state-of-the-art knowledge about office administration and all its functions

✔ Be able to plan, organize, and maintain productive work processes

✔ Be knowledgeable and experienced in the development and implementation of budgets

✔ Be well organized and skilled in working with the latest systems for records management, data storage, and bookkeeping

✔ Pay attention to detail and complete tasks with a high level of accuracy

✔ Be very effective at time management, prioritizing, and scheduling

✔ Be able to handle stress and work well under pressure

✔ Have the leadership ability to coordinate and manage the administrative team

Sales manager

Sales managers are responsible for directing an organization's sales programs and, depending on the size and nature of the organization, assigning sales territories, setting sales goals, and establishing training programs for sales representatives.

When you're customizing your strategic plan to include sales manager successors, keep in mind that the ideal sales manager should

✔ Have a high self-image and a positive outlook about the organization and its products and/or services

✔ Be able to lead, guide, and inspire outstanding performance from his or her sales team

- ✔ Be a skilled facilitator and trainer, with proven ability to teach, coach, and mentor his or her team, while also knowing what techniques will work best with which sales team members

- ✔ Be a persuasive communicator and a win-win negotiator

- ✔ Be able to form a constructive sales plan, schedule and implement it, measure its effectiveness, and quickly deal with any obstacles that get in the plan's way

- ✔ Have a high degree of knowledge and experience with the latest customer relationship management (CRM) systems

- ✔ Be able to read people by observing them and actively listening to their concerns with empathy and understanding

Shipping and receiving manager

Shipping and receiving managers oversee the receiving and shipping of products, including how they're handled, packaged, and processed.

When you're customizing your succession plan to include shipping and receiving manager successors, keep in mind that the ideal candidate should

- ✔ Be comfortable with multi-tasking, while at the same time paying close attention to detail

- ✔ Be skilled at time management and have a solid understanding of production scheduling and the ability to modify processes to meet scheduled deadlines

- ✔ Be highly organized with the ability to coordinate and expedite incoming and outgoing product movement

- ✔ Be able to train, organize, and coordinate his or her team to do hands-on work and ensure that shipping and delivery schedules are met and products are handled carefully and shipped or received accurately

- ✔ Be skilled at building relationships with vendors, negotiating costs, and scheduling deliveries

- ✔ Have strong follow-up skills, especially in terms of tracking, reporting on, and analyzing the status of products shipped and received

Other key positions

Most of this chapter is focused on leadership and management, without which organizations would flounder. However, depending on the size and type of your organization, there are other key positions in an organization that are essential to its success.

So, how do you go about identifying other key positions in your organization? Think about which positions would slow or even stop operations if they were vacated. These positions are held by employees who make a substantial contribution to the organization's operation, profitability, and success. For example:

- ✔ Someone who has information, knowledge, or expertise critical to some aspect of organizational functioning

- ✔ Someone who has developed an impressive network of sales and customer relationships

- ✔ Someone who has particularly helpful financial and banking relationships

- ✔ Someone who has special and useful industry contacts

Given the wide range of organizations, I can't give you a list of key positions that will match your specific needs. But here are a few examples:

- ✔ An executive assistant who has worked with the CEO for years and is uniquely experienced with all his or her habits, needs, and styles of doing work

- ✔ A star programmer whose unique creative ability to design and implement tailor-made programs has helped improve process efficiency or the flow of information in the organization

- ✔ An outstanding salesperson whose consistent high-level performance has significantly increased revenue, expanded the customer base, and enhanced the organization's reputation in the marketplace

- ✔ A brilliant accountant whose finely tuned skills, attention to detail, and knowledge about financial practices and principles has saved the organization money and greatly improved the bottom line

- ✔ A service mechanic in an automotive shop who has artfully solved a large variety of repair problems in a cost-effective and efficient manner and boosted the shop's reputation among customers

- ✔ A highly competent retail store manager whose knowledge of products and skills at promotions have led to customers flocking to the store, resulting in a dramatic increase in sales

- ✔ A very popular and personable receptionist who makes everyone he or she meets feel comfortable and important, and who adeptly steers people and incoming calls to the right person, which increases the organization's positive reputation and significantly contributes to operational efficiency

These are just examples. The important takeaway is to realize that there is more to customizing your succession plan than focusing exclusively on executives and managers who occupy key positions.

Looking Ahead: Fine-Tuning Your Plan for the Future

"Be prepared" has been the motto of the Boy Scouts for over a century. It also should be the motto of your succession-planning team as it works to help your organization anticipate the future.

Anticipating changes in the marketplace

When you're customizing your succession plan with an eye on the future, you need to anticipate changes in the marketplace. For example, what new positions or current employee competencies will you need in order to deal with events such as the following:

- ✔ New products and services emerging in the marketplace that are superior or more desirable to customers

- ✔ New and unexpected competition in the marketplace with streamlined production processes or creative marketing approaches

- ✔ New technologies that would help your organization be more effective in its operations and lead to improvements in the quality of the products or services you deliver

- ✔ Unexpected downturns in the economy that require new kinds of strategies and modifications in your products or services

- ✔ Impending demographic changes, such as the aging population, requiring major adjustments, additions, or discontinuation of various products and services offered by your organization

Keeping up with your strategic plan

Thinking about the future also means keeping up with your overall strategic plan. For example, what new positions and/or current employee competencies will you need in order to deal with the following changes in your overall strategic plan:

- ✔ A decision to significantly expand operations to markets in other parts of the world, which will require new, multicultural leadership competencies

✔ A decision to dramatically change a product line or the services you offer, which will require new kinds of operational expertise and marketing strategies

✔ A decision to restructure departments and operations in your organization, which will require new sets of personnel competencies

Making Sure Your Plan Meets Your Organization's Unique Needs

Step back for a moment and look at your organization as a whole. Think about it as one organization-wide team in which everyone, interdependently, is working together toward a set of common goals.

Being prepared for the departure of leaders and other key employees, including those strategically anticipated, is a first priority. However, all the other employees in your organization also make valuable contributions to its success in one way or another.

Here are just a few examples of the ways that various employees contribute to an organization's success:

✔ The delivery person who faithfully delivers your products without error and on schedule

✔ The accounts payable clerk who knows all the vendors and works hard at making sure all invoices are processed in a timely manner

✔ The administrative assistant who provides great help and support to various key managers by setting up meetings, helping with travel plans, and providing appropriate prompts and assistance to help keep projects and programs on schedule

✔ The custodian who keeps the work areas immaculate, responds immediately when needed, anticipates problems, and uses the most cost-effective steps and products in carrying out his or her responsibilities

You need to be prepared for the departure of any of these valuable employees. How well they do — even if their contributions are less significant than those of your key employees — will have a measurable impact on your organization's success.

Chapter 9

Figuring Out What You Need in a Successor

In This Chapter

▶ Understanding what competencies are

▶ Assessing the competencies needed for a particular position

▶ Forecasting what competencies will be needed in the future

*H*uman resources people and others interested in personnel selection and development use the word *competencies* to talk about what's required by someone to do a good job. The problem is, this term is the chameleon of HR and personnel development. Exactly what it means depends on who's using it.

Some people define *competencies* as "observable and measurable knowledge and skills." Others define it as "the characteristics that people have and use in ways to perform their jobs." Still other people use it to talk about the "expertise, experience, and abilities needed to do a good job." Yet, in spite of its vagueness, *competencies* is a popular and very widely used term in conversations about finding, selecting, hiring, developing, and promoting people in today's organizational world. In this chapter, I begin by giving you an easy-to-remember definition of *competencies*.

Why is the term *competencies* important to succession planning? Because the goal of succession planning is to find a successor who can step in and continue a job without missing a beat. In other words, the goal is to find a successor who has the right set of competencies to succeed. And that's what this chapter is all about.

What Are We Really Talking About When We Talk About Competencies?

A job consists of certain tasks that need to be completed. The personal characteristics needed by someone to complete those tasks well are *competencies.* So, what are competencies? The set of talents, aptitudes, skills, and knowledge needed by people to do their jobs.

To remember the definition of *competencies,* think of the acronym TASK:

- ✔ Talents
- ✔ Aptitudes
- ✔ Skills
- ✔ Knowledge

Talents

A *talent* is something you've always been able to do so easily and so naturally that you don't even see it as something special. Others may watch you doing it and say, "Wow, I wish I were as good as you are doing that!" But to you, it's just something you've been able to do all your life without even thinking about it.

Your talent isn't something you learned. It's an ability to do something or behave in a certain way that seems to be hard-wired into your very being. Here are some examples of talents:

- ✔ Even as a child, Ben was able to be completely at ease with a group of strangers. In fact, he often became the center of attention. Ben seems to have an innate ability to relate to people. He does it without even thinking.

- ✔ When Toiya was in school, she attended class after class, didn't take many notes, hardly studied at all, and yet consistently got A's. She has a natural academic talent.

- ✔ Kate can make everything beautiful without effort, from decorating her house to arranging a bouquet of flowers to setting the table for a dinner party. She has the talent to be artistic in everything she does. When asked, "Where did you learn to do that?" she simply replies, "I don't know — I've always been able to do it. I guess decorating just comes naturally to me."

When talented people are doing jobs that call for their special talents, the quality of their job performance soars, and their job satisfaction soars as well.

Aptitudes

For purposes of succession planning, consider an *aptitude* a kind of "baby talent." It's a natural characteristic that, when properly developed, can grow into a full-fledged talent. Here are some examples of aptitudes:

- ✔ Jennifer has always been naturally comfortable with numbers and calculations. She sailed through her math classes in high school without any effort. Then she went to college and grad school and earned an MBA degree. Jennifer's aptitude with numbers became highly developed. Now she's a talented chief financial officer.

- ✔ As early as Andrew can remember, he's always been good at organizing things. In fact, friends often teased him and called him obsessive-compulsive. After graduating from high school, Andrew started working in an office. Over the years, he gained a great deal of experience at office work and eventually moved up the chain to become a talented office manager.

- ✔ Since Gabe was 4 years old and received his first LEGO set, he's always enjoyed building and fixing things. After years of training and many apprentice experiences, he's now a successful, talented mechanical engineer.

There are probably many people in your organization with untapped aptitudes, people who, with some development and training, could assume other positions in which their flourishing talents could be brought to successful fruition, resulting in exceptional job performance.

Skills

Skills are an entirely different ballgame. Unlike talents and aptitudes, which people are born with, skills are things that people learn. Essentially, a skill is a behavior that someone develops through training and practice. You can't put talent into someone. But you can train people in order to develop particular skills, and every job has certain required skills. Here are some examples of skills:

- ✔ Damon has just acquired a brand-new computer system, but he really doesn't know how to operate it. So, he attends a weeklong training session to develop the skills he needs to operate the computer system.

✔ Juan would love to build a set of tables for his patio. But he's never had any experience at doing that. So, he attends a furniture-making class in which he learns how to build furniture. Now he has the skills to build the set of tables for his patio.

✔ Chloe didn't have much experience running a meeting before she became a manager, and she feels that her meetings aren't being run as effectively as they could. She decides to hire a consultant to train her on how to run effective meetings. After several training sessions, as she applies what she's learning, Chloe notices that the meetings are becoming much more efficient and productive. Now she has the skills to run an effective meeting.

When you're looking for a successor, you may start by looking for someone who already has the skills needed to do the job effectively. But don't rule out someone who doesn't have those skills, if he or she has demonstrated the ability to learn quickly.

Knowledge

Knowledge is the kind of information people need to know in order to perform their jobs effectively. Required knowledge comes in many shapes and sizes. It may be knowledge about a particular product. It may be knowledge about the capabilities and/or limitations of a particular piece of equipment. It may be knowledge about certain federal or state regulations that must be observed when performing their jobs. Here are some examples of knowledge that people may have:

✔ An auto dealer is offering a new car model to his customers. Not only is the new model electric, but it comes equipped with all the latest technology, including a GPS and a backup sensor. The salespeople need to be very knowledgeable about the new car and all its wonderful features to be effective at their jobs.

✔ State lawmakers have just established some new regulations with regard to hiring and firing employees. Everyone in the HR department must be knowledgeable about those regulations.

✔ Your organization has just gone global. You're now operating in a country with values, expectations, and customs entirely different from yours. You need to learn all about the people in that country in order to interact effectively with them.

Knowledge is a key component of competencies, but similar to skills, you can teach it.

Assessing Current Competencies

Determining the competencies needed for any particular job starts with knowing what you're looking for. And knowing what you're looking for means identifying the specific talents, aptitudes, skills, and knowledge that make up the competencies needed for anyone to perform and excel at the job.

Then when you consider various candidates for a position, you'll need to measure the degree to which they possess the required competencies.

The following steps give you a systematic process for determining and measuring competencies for any position you're focusing on in your succession plan.

Step 1: Identify job information resources

What you're looking for in this step are people who can provide you with descriptions of the competencies needed for the job. You may want to consult people who currently hold the position, people who held the position in the past, or other associates.

Step 2: Collect data

After identifying the resources who can get you the information you need, the next step is to tap them for ideas. This step involves identifying any job-related talents, aptitudes, skills, and knowledge:

- ✔ Observe people presently in the targeted positions as they perform their jobs.

- ✔ Interview people presently in those positions to find out what they think are the specific talents, aptitudes, skills, and knowledge needed to perform their jobs.

- ✔ Interview associates of the people presently in the positions to get their perceptions of what it takes to do the job.

- ✔ Interview people who previously occupied those positions.

- ✔ Discuss the position competency needs with people you may have access to through professional associations or relationships you've developed with people in other organizations with the same or similar positions.

- ✔ Review any published research and any other documents with information relevant to the position.

Step 3: Organize the data as you collect it

Organize your data into the following categories:

- **Talents:** What are the natural behaviors that would make people the best suited for the particular position you're looking at?

- **Aptitudes:** What aptitudes would allow you, with some training, coaching, and/or mentoring, to develop a successor from within your organization?

- **Skills:** What are the particular skills needed by a potential successor for the particular position you're looking at?

- **Knowledge:** What specific knowledge will be needed by (or at least be helpful to) someone assuming the vacant position?

Step 4: Develop interviewing guidelines for recognizing candidate competencies

Given all the data you've collected and organized, your next step is to specify the kinds of questions you should ask when meeting with potential successors.

How you structure an interview session and the kinds of questions you ask will depend on whether you're trying to determine the candidate's talents, aptitudes, skills, or knowledge.

Talents

Successfully identifying the candidate's talent during an interview is best accomplished by asking open-ended job-related questions. Open-ended questions allow candidates to go wherever they choose to go. Typically, these questions start with *who, what, where, when, why,* and *how,* and they can't be answered with a simple "yes" or "no." As a result, more often than not, candidates are likely to talk about areas in which they feel most comfortable and, thus, reveal information about their talents.

Aptitudes

Successfully identifying aptitudes during an interview is a little trickier. Because aptitudes are *potential* talents, you need to formulate questions that identify potentials.

Real-world example: A talent interview

I worked with an automobile dealer who was dedicated to delivering new vehicles to customers in top, pristine condition. To ensure that this would happen, he had a new car prep manager who supervised eight college students in getting the cars ready for delivery. Their responsibilities were to wash the cars, check every feature of the cars to make sure they were functioning correctly, and make sure the cars would be delivered in perfect condition. The dealer was very satisfied with the results he was getting from the new car prep manager and his team.

Then one day the manager came to him and told him he had to leave the dealership because his wife was taking a job in another state. The dealer was faced with hiring a new manager.

He decided to conduct a talent interview with candidates for the manager position. I asked him to tell me what talents he was looking for. He told me he needed someone who was good with people, because the young college students in the prep department were a "bundle to handle." He also wanted someone who was very, very good at details, because he wanted every car to be delivered to a customer in "absolutely perfect condition."

So, we started interviewing candidates. After interviewing several people. We found someone who seemed to fill the bill. Among the series of open-ended questions we asked him, was, "I noticed from your résumé that you've held four different jobs in the last ten years. Of those jobs, which did you like best and why?"

He responded, "Gee, that's a difficult question for me to answer."

"Why?" we asked.

"Well," he said, "I've been very lucky. In every job I've had, I've worked with some wonderful people. And that's one of the most important things I look for in a job."

Bingo. He met the dealer's first requirement: a talent to relate to people.

Later in the interview, we asked him another question: "What kind of activity gives you the most satisfaction when you're working at a job?"

"I love to organize things," he answered. "In fact," he said, continuing with a smile, "my wife calls me a neat freak! She's so unorganized! When she comes home and takes off her coat and shoes, she leaves them all over the place, and I always have to pick up after her. When she washes dishes, she never really gets them clean and I have to redo them. She just doesn't pay attention to detail!"

Another bingo! The dealer now had someone who met his second requirement: paying attention to detail.

Not surprisingly, the dealer hired him as the new car prep manager. Six months later, I asked the dealer how it was working out. He told me this was one of the best hires he had ever made.

For example, you may ask, "If you could do anything you wanted to do, no strings attached, what would you choose?" This question may reveal an existing talent, but it also could tell you something about a candidate's aptitude that could be developed into a full-blown talent.

Another set of questions may be, "Tell me about a stressful situation you've been in at work. How did you deal with it, and if you had to deal with it again would you do anything different?" Here again, you may identify an aptitude that could be developed into a full-blown talent.

Skills

Determining a candidate's skills during an interview is much easier than determining talents or aptitudes. In this case, the questions are simply straightforward questions about skills needed for the job.

For example, suppose you're looking for a new IT manager. You may ask the candidate technical questions that would indicate how much he or she knows about operating a particular kind of computer system or using a specific program.

As another example, you may be looking for a person to coordinate a strategic-planning team, consisting of people with very committed ideas and positions that lead them into frequent conflict with one another. You may give candidates an example of a conflict in a team meeting and ask them how they would resolve it. Their answer may tell you if they have any conflict-resolution skills.

Knowledge

Determining a candidate's knowledge during an interview is much easier than determining talents or aptitudes. In this case, you know the kind of knowledge a candidate should have to be able to qualify for the successor position. In the interview, you then simply ask questions that require such knowledge and see how the candidate responds.

Step 5: Develop rating scales to use when interviewing a candidate

Ideally, you should have more than one person interview a successor candidate, especially if the position is a key leadership position or some other technical position very critical to the company's future. But when more than one person interviews a potential successor, you need some method for weighing their impressions of the candidate.

For example, suppose you're interviewing candidates to find a successor for your star salesman who has decided to leave your organization. You meet with your sales managers to identify a list of competencies and develop interview questions.

Then, because you're asking more than one person to interview every candidate, you develop a rating scale, like the one shown in Figure 9-1. Using this kind of rating scale will help you determine the degree of agreement among the interviewers and, along with interviewer observations, will enable you to select the right candidate.

| Name of Candidate: _____ _____ Date: ___/___/___ |
| Last   First |

Name of Rater: _____ _____
Last First

	1	2	3	4	5

1. Not just looking for a job, looking for a career—sees what he does as a 24 hour life style.
   UNACCEPTABLE ◄──────► OUTSTANDING

2. Shows passion and enthusiasm about what he does—sees it as having fun.
   UNACCEPTABLE ◄──────► OUTSTANDING

3. Is driven to do well, to be competent, the best at what he does—has the ability to learn and apply what he learns.
   UNACCEPTABLE ◄──────► OUTSTANDING

4. Sets goals and sticks to them.
   UNACCEPTABLE ◄──────► OUTSTANDING

5. The desire to win over a customer, to succeed at his job, is more important than money.
   UNACCEPTABLE ◄──────► OUTSTANDING

6. Is a good problem-solver in overcoming objections.
   UNACCEPTABLE ◄──────► OUTSTANDING

7. Goes out of his way to help everyone.
   UNACCEPTABLE ◄──────► OUTSTANDING

8. Is a good communicator, particularly a good listener.
   UNACCEPTABLE ◄──────► OUTSTANDING

9. Exhibits maturity in the choices and decisions he has made.
   UNACCEPTABLE ◄──────► OUTSTANDING

10. Has a strong work ethic and is good at handling stress.
    UNACCEPTABLE ◄──────► OUTSTANDING

11. Gets along well with people and has a likeable and engaging personality.
    UNACCEPTABLE ◄──────► OUTSTANDING

12. Is a team player.
    UNACCEPTABLE ◄──────► OUTSTANDING

Figure 9-1: A rating scale for interviewing salespeople.

Looking At Competencies for Key Positions

Working through the steps in the previous section, you can come up with a set of competencies for any of the key positions identified in your succession plan. Depending on the nature and size of your organization, you may not be able to invest the money and time needed to carry out all these steps for all positions in as much detail as you would like, but you should concentrate on collecting as much of the TASK data as possible.

In this section, I offer some examples of assessed competencies for key positions. Even though your organization may have more unique competency needs for these positions, you'll find many of these suggested competencies relevant to your own succession plan.

Top leadership competencies

Here are some examples of competencies shared by many top leaders in a variety of organizations resulting from a TASK assessment:

- **Charisma:** Have you ever seen anyone walk into a room and almost immediately become the center of attention? This is a natural talent shared by many top leaders.

- **Ability to inspire:** The ability to inspire others, to stimulate their enthusiasm for a particular goal or project, is essential in a leader.

- **Vision:** Vision is about having a clear picture of the future in mind and knowing how to get there.

- **Strategic thinking:** When making decisions and taking actions, a leader stays focused on the implications of any future changes for the organization.

- **Communication skills:** A leader should effectively communicate at every level, from individuals to large groups.

- **Decisiveness:** A leader easily makes decisions with the confidence that they're the right decisions.

- **Perseverance:** A leader continues to work hard at accomplishing a goal, in spite of what looks to be insurmountable obstacles.

- **Integrity:** A leader is trustworthy and honest, has ethical intentions, and can be depended upon to be fair in all situations.

- **Business expertise:** A leader has accumulated knowledge about what makes a business successful, including organizational structures, finances, staffing, efficient processes, marketing, competitors, and so on.

- **Product or service knowledge:** A leader is knowledgeable and up to date about the product or service being offered by the organization.

In addition to top leadership positions, your organization may have several other kinds of management positions. See Chapter 8 for examples of the kinds of competencies you may identify for those positions.

Competencies for other key positions

In the broadest view of succession planning, every position is a possible key position. You may have an indispensable IT specialist who knows exactly how to quickly fix a computer hardware or software problem whenever it occurs. You may have a receptionist who excels at making people feel comfortable when they come into your organization.

From this perspective, the more broadly your succession plan is developed in describing position competencies, the more beneficial it will be to your organization. In the following sections, I provide a few examples you can customize for your own organization.

Computer programmer

Computer programmers are responsible for developing programs designed for specific projects, such as the analysis of customer feedback surveys, the analysis of job performance reviews, creating periodic sales reports, and so on. In a computer programmer, you need the following competencies:

- ✔ **Analytical and conceptual skills:** A computer programmer should be able to quickly grasp what is needed and conceptualize the components of a program to meet the need.

- ✔ **Logical problem-solving skills:** A computer programmer should be able to grasp what's going wrong when a program isn't working the way it's supposed to work and effectively debugging it.

- ✔ **Programming skills:** A computer programmer has the ability to develop efficient and user-friendly programs using the latest programming language.

- ✔ **Writing skills:** A computer programmer should be able to write an easy-to-use manual for people using any of the programs created.

- ✔ **Training skills:** A computer programmer should be able to train people to use programs that have been created.

- ✔ **Computer knowledge:** A computer programmer should have knowledge of all aspects of computers, including programming language, major operating systems, software used in the organization, and computer hardware.

Receptionist

Receptionists are positioned at the entrance of the organization to greet visitors and answer phone calls. In a receptionist, you need the following competencies:

- **Excellent interpersonal skills:** A receptionist acknowledges people who come into the organization in a courteous and friendly manner.

- **Positive attitude:** A receptionist radiates optimism and cheerfulness in the eyes of people calling or coming into the organization.

- **Helpfulness:** A receptionist is motivated to help people, giving priority to satisfying people by making sure they get what they want.

- **Ability to multi-task:** A receptionist is able to handle several calls at once, while at the same time talking to and helping people who walk through the door.

- **Ability to manage stress:** A receptionist can handle the stress of many calls and visits simultaneously, without falling apart.

- **Excellent memory:** A receptionist can remember the names and faces of people, including visitors as well as employees.

- **Attention to detail:** A receptionist is accurate and detailed in the timely transmission of messages to people in the organization.

Customer service representative

Customer service representatives deal with customer calls ranging from questions about products or services to complaints and other customer problems. In a customer service representative, you need the following competencies:

- **Self-confidence:** A customer service rep should be confident that with patience, a little time, and the right approach, he or she can handle any customer situation.

- **Problem-solving mindset:** A customer service rep should have the desire to help customers in solving any problems they have, along with the ability to come up with satisfying solutions.

- **Solid communication skills:** A customer service rep should be able to communicate clearly, tactfully, and persuasively.

- **Emotional control:** A customer service rep should be able to communicate calmly and logically, even when talking to customers who are upset. Customer service reps should be able to deal with distressed customers who are very upset without themselves losing their cool.

✔ **Ability to handle rejection:** A customer service rep should be able to hear customers scream and even curse at him or her, or hang up on him or her, without taking it personally.

✔ **Great listening skills:** A customer service rep should be able to listen actively to customers, help them clarify their orders or issues, and ultimately cause customers to feel that they're truly being heard.

✔ **Upbeat attitude:** A customer service rep should be able to reflect a positive and enthusiastic attitude when speaking on the phone.

✔ **Accuracy:** A customer service rep should be able to gather full information from the customers and accurately enter their orders and document the process as needed.

HR facilitator

The facilitator in the HR department is assigned the job of facilitating team meetings to make sure they're conducted efficiently and productively. Facilitators are catalysts to teams — they guide a group in getting its work done. In an HR facilitator, you need the following competencies:

✔ **Knowledge of group dynamics:** An HR facilitator should have an understanding of the behavior of people in groups, group norms, conformity, conflict resolution, and so on.

✔ **Skill at running meetings:** An HR facilitator should know how to guide meetings, keeping them efficient and focused on the tasks at hand while the team engages in productive problem solving and decision making.

✔ **The ability to withhold judgment:** An HR facilitator should remain neutral about everything he or she hears. While facilitating, the facilitator suspends his or her own beliefs and assumptions. The facilitator hears only words and ideas without any judgments. This frame of mind is essential for a facilitator, because it keeps the discussions robust and maintains an atmosphere that is highly receptive to creative thinking.

✔ **Objectivity:** An HR facilitator should act as a third party, striving to be unbiased and neutral, focusing on meeting content only when it repeats itself, goes in circles, doesn't stay in focus, and so on.

✔ **The ability to actively listen:** An HR facilitator should immediately and accurately capture (clarifying when necessary) the essence of ideas offered by team members without interfering with the flow of the discussion.

✔ **Sensitivity to nonverbal cues:** An HR facilitator continuously observes voice intonations and inflections, facial expressions, body language, and so on. He or she can infer from these observations whether someone is being defensive, irritated, or withdrawn.

✔ **Diplomacy:** An HR facilitator is able to diplomatically handle such behaviors as defensiveness, irritation, and hostility by using patience, tact, and even humor to maintain the team climate.

✔ **Skill in using problem-solving tools:** An HR facilitator is skilled in applying a variety of problem-solving strategies and process improvement techniques, such as flowcharting, brainstorming, force-field analysis, mind mapping, action planning, and so on.

Purchasing manager

The purchasing manager oversees the centralized purchasing functions of the organization, including contract negotiation and administration, equipment and supply purchases, preparation of financial reports for managers, and so on. In a purchasing manager, you need the following competencies:

✔ **Organization skills:** A purchasing manager should be able to plan, organize, direct, and coordinate the work of his or her team.

✔ **Negotiation skills:** A purchasing manager should be able to negotiate purchases with vendors that are cost saving, without sacrificing quality, and to ensure vendor contract compliance.

✔ **Analytical ability:** A purchasing manager should be able to analyze procurement requirements and determine procurement procedures.

✔ **Solid communication skills:** A purchasing manager should be able to communicate clearly and concisely, both orally and in writing, including the preparation of clear and concise financial reports.

✔ **Relationship-building skills:** A purchasing manager should be able to establish and maintain effective working relationships with people throughout the organization, as well as relationships with external contacts such as vendors.

✔ **Purchasing expertise:** A purchasing manager should have an in-depth understanding of principles, practices, and applications of purchasing, budget preparation, and federal, state, and local codes, laws, and regulations particularly relevant to the purchasing function.

Production engineer

The production engineer in a manufacturing organization represents the manufacturing department at customer and product development meetings and is responsible for making sure that the design of new products is in sync with customer needs, as well as production capabilities and capacities. In a production engineer, you need the following competencies:

- ✔ **Manufacturing and production expertise:** A production engineer should know how to interpret technical drawings and the steps needed to meet hardware, manufacturing, and operational needs.

- ✔ **The desire to be a team player:** A production manager should be able to develop a strong team culture throughout the production department and strengthen the abilities of team members to work more effectively as a team.

- ✔ **A willingness to collaborate:** A production manager should be able to collaborate effectively and productively with people, representing the manufacturing department in meetings at all levels of the organization.

- ✔ **Attention to detail:** A production manager should be able to design clear and detailed production goals, as well as the plans and strategies to meet them on time.

- ✔ **Innovativeness:** A production manager should be able to create and implement more efficient methods in the production line.

- ✔ **Problem-solving skills:** A production manager should be able to quickly and efficiently come up with solutions to a wide range of production problems. He or she should be very knowledgeable about process improvement techniques, monitor all aspects of production, and provide training, coaching, and guidance to continually improve operations.

Determining Future Competencies

Strategic plans change. Customer needs and preferences change. Market conditions change. Even after you've determined the competencies needed for key positions, more likely than not, you'll have to modify them or expand them to adapt to such changes.

Whether changes are the result of revisions to your overall strategic plan or the result of changes or anticipated changes in the marketplace, your succession-planning team has to be prepared at a moment's notice to revise sets of competencies for key positions.

For example, consider key leadership and management positions. Never before have changes in organizational management and operations occurred as quickly or as dramatically as they're happening today on a global level. New technologies and the ways people communicate with one another are in a constant state of change. Consumers are shopping differently for products and services than they did years ago. Increasingly, purchases are made and services are contracted online. In addition, consumers use online resources to find ratings and feedback about the quality of products and services offered. Manufacturing jobs, customer service jobs, and technical support jobs are being outsourced to other countries. Not only are organizations more globally connected, but they're also located in multiple places around the world.

These kinds of developments call for changes in existing competency sets for leaders and managers or (at the very least) changes in the relative importance of some competencies over others. Here are some examples:

- ✔ In today's changing world, leaders and managers need to be more flexible than ever before. This adds or at least emphasizes flexibility as a key leader and manager competency. Leaders and managers need to be very adaptable and ready to change practices, procedures, and programs as quickly as possible.

- ✔ Given the way technology is changing business operations and consumer behavior, increased emphasis will need to be placed on innovativeness" as a key competency. In today's world, it's the organizations that dramatically innovate that rise to the top.

- ✔ This increased emphasis on innovativeness as a key competency for leaders and managers will help foster an organization-wide culture that supports employee ideas, input, and creative thinking.

Be alert to similar revisions in other key positions in your organization. You need to be ready, willing, and able to quickly and effectively adapt to change.

Today's innovator

In today's world of online marketing, Zappos (www.zappos.com) has emerged as one of the most innovative companies in the world when it comes to connecting with and satisfying customers. CEO Tony Hsieh decided that rather than using his resources to fund advertising as typical companies do, he would focus on making customers happy. The result: incredibly high levels of customer retention.

Hsieh has used Internet technology to connect with Zappos customers in some highly innovative ways. He offers customers free overnight shipping, free return shipping, and 24/7 company operations to process orders and care for customers. He has a warehouse with 70 robots that enable him to ship a pair of shoes in as little as eight minutes.

Customer service personnel are encouraged to make decisions on their own. For example, they can offer a refund on a defective item without having to ask for the approval of a manager. They're asked to send at least a dozen personal notes to customers every day, and they're encouraged to make personal, emotional connections with customers.

Focused on making customers and employees happy, Hsieh has created an entirely new kind of corporate structure and culture. A new Zappos employee receives two weeks of classroom training and then spends two additional weeks learning how to answer customer calls. By the time employees have worked at Zappos for two years, they'll have received more than 200 hours of class time during work hours and they will have read nine business books.

Hsieh offers employees additional classes in public speaking, as well as courses in financial planning to those who do well in the earlier training. His goal is to provide people with training and mentorship that will enable them to become senior leaders within the company.

He treats his employees in restaurants and bars to give them an opportunity to "hang out together." His aim is to create a culture in which everyone is friends with everyone else. Dedicated to building a fun, loose work environment, he requires managers to spend 10 percent to 20 percent of their time "goofing off" with the people they manage. Hsieh's premise is that if you create a little fun and a little weirdness in the corporate culture, it will encourage people to deliver a "wow" experience to customers. Finally, to get employees to think about the meaning of their work, every year they're asked to write a fresh essay for a book on the subject of the company's culture, which he publishes and distributes to all the staff.

Looking beyond competencies

Competencies aren't everything when it comes to hiring a successor. You may find someone who has just the right combination of talents, aptitudes, skills, and knowledge, but who doesn't have enough experience or doesn't mesh well with your organization's culture. Consider the following as you interview candidates:

✔ **Experience:** Experience is an important ingredient to throw into the hiring pot. All the elements of TASK — talents, aptitudes, skills, and knowledge — are seasoned by experience. Experience itself is not a competency, but it enriches the competencies a candidate has.

✔ **Cultural fit:** To determine whether a candidate will fit your organizational culture, you need to know what you're referring to when you talk about your organizational culture. For purposes of succession planning, think about your organizational culture in terms of its work environment, the way it's structured, the way business is conducted, and how employees are treated. (For more on organizational culture, see Chapter 10.)

An awareness of the key elements of your organizational culture gives you a framework for shaping some of the questions to ask a potential successor during the interview, such as "Tell me about the best manager you've ever worked for and why you think he or she was the best" or "How would you describe your ideal work environment?" or "What are you looking for in a colleague or co-worker?"

Although these questions aren't tapping competencies, they can give you a glimpse of how well the candidate will fit into your organizational culture. The better the fit, the more likely your candidate will do an outstanding job.

Chapter 10

Identifying and Developing Successors within Your Organization

In This Chapter

▶ Laying the foundation with a competency culture

▶ Helping employees develop and grow

▶ Reinforcing your competency culture every step of the way

Succession planning is all about finding successors for key positions. Easier said than done, though. Finding those people is a major challenge for any organization. The first impulse of many organizations is to look outside the organization to fill key positions. They start with a recruiting agency or an executive search firm. ("Heck, they know what they're doing!") Run an ad. ("You're bound to get some responses.") Network with friends and associates in professional associations. ("They may know someone.")

It's true: All these options are potentially effective sources for successors. But don't limit yourself by looking only outside your organization. Too many organizations don't work hard enough to identify potential successors on the inside — namely, the currently employed individuals who are familiar with your organizational culture. Many of your current employees may have the competencies you need — or at least have the potential to develop them with additional coaching, guidance, and training. In the end, identifying internal successors and providing the necessary training and development may be far less expensive and time-consuming than looking outside the organization. That's what this chapter is all about.

The word *competencies* refers to talents, aptitudes, skills, and knowledge (see Chapter 9).

Creating a Competency Culture

Before you identify and develop people within your organization as potential candidates to meet the needs of your succession plan, take a moment to consider your organizational culture. For purposes of succession planning, think about your organizational culture in terms of its work environment, how it's structured, the way business is conducted, and how employees are treated.

You can get a quick sense of the most important elements of your organizational culture by asking yourself a few simple questions:

- ✔ **How are decisions made in your organization?** Do they require successive steps of approval up the chain of command? To what extent are employees empowered to make decisions at every level?

- ✔ **How structured is your organization?** Are there clear, hierarchical lines of authority? Or is it a more horizontal, flat, and loosely structured organization?

- ✔ **How would you describe the general mindset of employees in your organization?** Do they have a cooperative, problem-solving mindset, or is there a lot of finger pointing and blaming when things go wrong?

- ✔ **How would you describe the way people work in your organization?** Is there a lot of open communication and collaborative teamwork, or is it a highly competitive working climate?

- ✔ **How are employees rewarded when they do something right?** How are they treated when they do something wrong?

When you have a sense of the overall culture of your organization, home in on how competencies are treated: What kind of culture do you have when it comes to competencies? Your organization will be more successful if it incorporates a *competency culture*. So, what exactly is a competency culture, and how do you know if it exists in your organization? Here's a simple checklist of how people feel and behave in a competency culture:

- ✔ People believe their organization cares about them and wants them to be happy and competent at what they do.

- ✔ People feel that their job is important to the success of the organization and believe that management shares that view.

- ✔ People have a learning mindset. They're always open to acquiring new information and learning new skills that will help them develop their competencies and improve the quality of their work as well as their overall productivity.

✔ People see their organization encouraging and supporting their learning mindset by offering coaching, mentoring, training, and other educational opportunities to help them develop their competencies.

✔ People believe they'll have opportunities to be promoted or transferred to positions that make full use of their competencies.

✔ People are motivated and feel free to do whatever it takes to deliver the high-quality work and service needed to satisfy both internal and external customers.

✔ People value teamwork. Collaborating with one another, within and between departments, they see themselves as being interrelated and working as one organization-wide team in pursuit of the organization's mission.

Succession plans flourish in organizations with competency cultures. There is never any shortage of potential candidates to become successors for vacated or new positions.

If you suspect that your organization falls short of being a competency culture, take the steps described in this chapter to develop the competencies of potential successors within your organization. You'll strengthen the foundation and future of your organization.

Developing Current Employees' Competencies

Mining the field of potential successor candidates from within your organization to meet the needs of your succession plan involves several steps. These steps will take hours of effort and cost money. But in the long run, this investment of time and money will be beneficial to your organization in several ways:

✔ It sends a message to everyone in the organization that employees are valued, which contributes to higher morale.

✔ It shows people other opportunities within the organization, which increases employee retention.

✔ It saves time in orienting and training new employees and familiarizing them with your organization and its culture.

✔ Employees are more motivated to perform high-quality work, collaborate with others, and provide outstanding services to their customers because they see the possibility of promotions or transfers to other desirable positions.

✔ The stronger the emphasis put on internal searches, the more people will understand gaps between their current competencies and the competencies they need to get the jobs they want — and the more likely they'll be to do their best at developing needed competencies, so they can move to those desired positions.

✔ Given the emphasis put on competencies in internal development, the performance assessment process will be easier.

A key end result of all this is increased productivity.

In the following sections, I walk you through how to develop current employees' competencies so that when you have an open position, you have a qualified pool of potential successors down the hall.

Identifying potential successors

The first step in developing competencies is identifying people within your organization who have the potential, with some development, to fill key positions when they become vacant.

To identify a potential successor for a position, you need to know what competencies are required for the position (see Chapter 9).

After you've specified the competencies needed for a specific position, you're ready to identify potential candidates. Here's how:

✔ **Look at how people are performing in their current jobs.** Current job performance is the best indicator of potential. In particular look at the following:

• **Performance reviews:** The day-to-day performance of people will reflect their competencies.

• **The quality of their work:** Do you see evidence of the kind of person you want in the position?

• **How they work:** Observe employees on the job, and look for evidence of the competencies you need.

• **Their reputation:** Listen to what fellow employees, customers, vendors, and others say about them.

✔ **Get suggestions from managers.** Managers are the ones who know your organization's employees the best — they're in the trenches with them day in and day out.

Don't make consulting with managers the *only* way you identify a potential successor. Some managers may have personal biases.

✓ **Listen to the employees themselves.** Many times, when employees become aware of an opening they're interested in, they talk about it and let people know they're interested.

✓ **Determine the level of employees' motivation.** Have they pursued any training and development on their own? How excited are they about possible promotions or transfers in the future?

No matter how you identify potential candidates, you need to have a solid understanding of the kinds of competencies you're seeking. Every position has its own unique set of desirable competencies. In some cases, interpersonal talent is needed. In others, technical skills are a must. In still others, expertise in a particular field of knowledge is required. Those specific competencies, or at least some signs of employee aptitudes for them, will be what you're looking for.

Having a highly developed competency culture, in which competencies have been carefully specified for everyone and stored in your employee database, will help you identify potential candidates much more efficiently and rapidly. All you'll need to do for your first step is to conduct a computer search.

After you've identified people as potential candidates, the next step is to make an assessment of the kinds of support they need to become fully qualified candidates. This means creating individual development plans for them and determining the learning activities that will best prepare them.

Creating individual development plans

An *individual development plan* is a strategy for helping an employee develop the competencies needed to assume a new position. It's basically a comparison of current competencies to needed competencies, followed by a specific description of the kinds of learning experiences needed by the candidate to develop the required competencies.

Follow these steps to create an individual development plan:

1. **Specify the competencies needed for the new position.**

   What talents, aptitudes, skills, and knowledge (TASK) will be needed by the candidate to perform well in the new position? (See Chapter 9 for the definition of competencies and more on TASK.)

2. **Assess the current competencies of the candidate.**

3. **Compare the two sets of competencies to identify any gaps between them.**

4. **Determine the kinds of learning activities that will be needed by the candidate to close any gaps.**

5. **Specify learning objectives for each of the developmental activities.**

   These objectives will help you evaluate the level of success in preparing your candidate for the new position.

Providing in-house training

Many larger organizations have full-fledged HR departments that design and conduct training and development programs to help people develop their competencies. This typically calls for an experienced trainer or training director who knows how to create and deliver a training program. An alternative is to hire a training consultant who will help you create and implement such a program.

In-house training has several advantages:

- ✔ People don't have to travel to training sessions, so they aren't wasting valuable time in transit.

- ✔ Training sessions can be timed in ways that are convenient for individual work schedules.

- ✔ With no travel time and convenient scheduling, in-house training is less expensive.

- ✔ Work activities aren't disrupted as much as they are when employees have to leave work.

- ✔ Unlike external training programs, in-house trainers will be more focused on and tailored to your employees' specific training needs.

- ✔ Because internal training is fully immersed in the organizational culture, it offers attendees examples of behaviors and performance that are familiar to them.

- ✔ An in-house training program sends a message to employees that having the right competencies is important, and your organization is willing to invest time and resources in their development.

On the other hand, in-house training does have a few disadvantages:

✔ To start with, if you don't already have a training and development program, the cost to establish one is substantial. Depending on the size and nature of your organization, you have to weigh those costs against the long-term benefits and cost savings.

✔ Using in-house trainers opens you up to the risk of passing on current bad working habits to other people.

✔ Some staff may not take the training as seriously as they would if they were sent to a workshop or some other training session. They may see external trainers as having more expertise than people within their own organization.

If you don't already have the capacity for in-house training and development capability, but you'd like to establish one for your employees, here are some suggestions:

✔ Retain a trainer who is experienced at designing, conducting, and evaluating training programs to direct and coordinate the training function.

✔ Set up the infrastructure (equipment, materials, and facility) for conducting training sessions.

✔ Have the training specialist conduct a needs analysis to determine and prioritize the areas in which additional training is needed, as well as the best ways to provide it.

✔ Depending on the competencies involved, the training director may need to bring in experts to help design and even deliver training.

✔ Think about the trainees as if they were your customers and think of the training as a service you're offering. What kinds of experiences and exercises can you offer that will satisfy them?

✔ Define very clear learning objectives that can be used at the end of training to assess its effectiveness.

✔ At every opportunity, tie the competencies that are being developed to the organizational mission.

✔ Build in a request for participant feedback, which, along with the assessment results, will help you improve your future training programs.

Although an in-house training program can be very useful to your organization, much of the training needed by a potential candidate can be accomplished with coaches, mentors, and giving people assigned projects as described in the following sections. So, don't be discouraged if your organization can't swing a full training program right now.

Coaching and mentoring people

Coaching potential successors means helping them first identify which competencies need improvement and/or development and then helping them develop those competencies. Whether the coach is one of your managers, a training specialist from the HR department, or an outside consultant, the coach should be:

- **A good communicator:** You want someone who is able to clearly express ideas and instructions and is an empathetic, active listener.

- **Perceptive:** The coach should be skilled in identifying the gaps between where a person is now and where that person needs to be, and then be able to translate those gaps into specific goals that must be achieved.

- **A problem solver:** You need someone who treats every problem as an opportunity to teach the candidate how to develop the competencies needed to overcome it.

- **Patient:** The coach should understand that a coaching session won't always go as smoothly as desired. He or she shouldn't get upset when training glitches arise; instead, the coach should calmly help the candidate continue to learn, develop, and grow.

- **Effective at giving constructive feedback:** A coach needs to be able to let candidates know exactly what kind of progress they're making without discouraging them.

Managers play an important role in coaching potential candidates. In a competency culture, the most important job of a manager is to bring out the best in his or her employees. Coaching helps them do that.

When it comes to succession planning, managers often are the first people to spot a potential candidate for an open position. After all, they're constantly guiding and monitoring the performance of their employees. Their coaching skills play a key role in your succession plan because such skills are particularly useful in developing potential candidates:

- Managers are in the position to inspire potential candidates and motivate them to take on the challenge of new learning and personal development.

- Managers are the people most in touch with the candidate's work and most intimately knowledgeable about his or her competencies, which makes it easier for them to identify the training gaps and set coaching goals.

✔ Having already established a relationship with a potential candidate, a manager's encouragement to learn and grow is far more likely to be heard and followed.

✔ Knowing the candidate, managers know just the right questions to ask to help potential candidates think things through.

✔ As their manager, complimenting or praising the candidate for progress is especially meaningful.

Mentoring is similar to coaching. However, there are some significant differences:

✔ Whereas coaches work at directing people toward specific goals and advising them along the way, mentors are more like role models. They're facilitators who help the candidate develop the competencies he or she has.

✔ Think of coaches more broadly as people who motivate, inspire, and teach people. Think of mentors as people who the candidate follows, working alongside them and learning from them.

✔ Coaches are experts who educate employees, teaching them how to develop themselves. Mentors are people the employees want to emulate in order to become as competent as the mentors are.

In succession planning, you can assign coaches to help a potential candidate develop the competencies needed for the position. Or, you can assign potential candidates to work alongside employees who either hold the position that is about to be vacated or are very familiar with it. The idea behind the mentoring approach is that candidates can learn a lot simply by observing.

Giving special assignments

You don't have to send employees out to attend training programs and workshops to develop competencies. You can give people assignments that will help develop competencies. For example:

✔ **Assign people to tasks that will allow them to develop the needed competencies.** For example, suppose you have a successful salesperson who you're considering for a sales manager position. Give that person the job of developing a sales training manual that gives new salespeople tips and techniques, based on his or her experiences.

✔ **Assign people to a committee that will allow them to broaden their present competencies.** For example, suppose you have a customer service representative who you're thinking about promoting to a customer service supervisor. Assign that operator to a committee charged with the task of monitoring incoming calls and providing the other representatives with training and coaching to improve their telephone skills.

✔ **Rotate people to other jobs that will help them learn and practice the competencies needed for a new position.** For example, suppose your organization is global and you're looking at a candidate to succeed a manager located in another culture. Send that manager to the other location with an assignment to complete a specific project that will involve the help of people in that culture.

✔ **Give people assignments that will show them new ways of doing things.** For example, suppose you're looking to fill a position being vacated by a key engineer whose innovations have improved several products. Ask the candidate to visit competitors to find out how and why they do what they do.

✔ **Give people information-acquisition assignments.** For example, suppose you're considering a candidate to fill a key HR position dealing with changes in current regulations. Assign that person the task of reviewing and preparing a report on current local, state, and federal employment regulations and their relevance to your organization.

Not only will such assignments be helpful in developing candidate competencies, but they'll also yield work products helpful to the organization.

When assigning candidates to such activities, make sure they're coached and/or mentored on a regular basis throughout the duration of the assignment (see the preceding section).

Sending employees to professional association meetings

Regardless of the competencies you're trying to develop in your employees, there's bound to be an association relevant to that job (for example, the Association of Information Technology Professionals or the Society for Human Resource Management). And associations often have meetings (nationally, locally, or both), where attendees can listen to presentations, network with other people in the field, and pick up information that can help them develop professionally.

Sending candidates to professional association meetings can help them develop their competencies in many ways:

- ✔ It can increase a candidate's knowledge.

- ✔ It can give candidates opportunities to meet peers, some of whom may have a more developed set of competencies that can be instructional.

- ✔ It can increase a candidate's understanding of the particular business or mission of his or her organization.

- ✔ It can be a source of members-only articles and online resources that will be helpful to the candidate in developing competencies.

- ✔ It can introduce the candidate to contacts who can be a source of new ideas and new ways of doing things.

- ✔ It can give candidates the chance to update their knowledge and skills through seminars.

- ✔ It can link candidates to experts in the field who can help your organization develop more effective internal training.

Encouraging employees to go back to school

Today's educational system is going through a major change. Colleges and universities used to be focused on very rigorous academic training. More and more, educational institutions are focusing on graduating what are called *scholar-practitioners,* people who learn about new theories, research, and other information in their chosen field, and get experience applying that knowledge to solving problems and improving practices in their own profession.

Many institutions are attracting people who are immersed in their chosen careers and want to advance themselves, their knowledge, and their work skills. These institutions are designing programs suited to people who are busily balancing their work and home lives. Some programs offer MBAs or master's degrees in organizational development and leadership.

Several outstanding executive MBA programs cater specifically to fully employed people. The classes are held during evenings and/ or weekends, and they provide an excellent opportunity for potential successors for key positions to develop and strengthen a wide range of managerial and leadership skills. A sampling of these programs Some examples include the Ross Executive MBA Program at

the University of Michigan (www.bus.umich.edu/Admissions/
EMBA/Whyross.htm), the New York University Stern Executive
MBA Program (www.stern.nyu.edu/programs-admissions/
executive-mba/index.htm), the UCLA Anderson Executive
MBA Program (www.anderson.ucla.edu/emba.xml), and
the University of Pennsylvania Wharton Executive MBA Program
(www.wharton.upenn.edu/mbaexecutive).

Online resources

Your organization can develop people's competencies online. Some larger organizations have the capabilities to develop their own internal online training, while other organizations that lack such capabilities depend on external online training. Given today's continuing explosion of information sharing via the Internet and social media, online training is becoming more and more popular.

There are several advantages to using online training:

✔ **Online training is less costly.** You don't have to invest in the physical resources needed for a training facility. There are no traveling and accommodations costs involved in online training (this is especially true for organizations that have global locations). There's no need to spend money on developing training materials, because anything needed for the training will be online.

✔ **Online training offers more flexibility.** People may not have the time to go to a scheduled session. But online they can access the training at any time, day or night. People can finish the training at their own pace, as long as they do so in time to be considered as a potential successor. Some people are faster learners than others, so flexibility also allows people to progress at their own paces. People can access the training from any location, using a variety of new technologies in addition to computers, such as smartphones and iPads.

✔ **Assessments of learning effectiveness are more effective and efficient.** Learning assessments can be made more interactive, including potential scenarios or case analyses. Assessments are conducted online using questionnaires and/or exercises, and trainees get immediate feedback.

Online training programs can be developed within the organization or offered from external sources. Professional associations offer online resources. Many independent training sites offer online instruction as well.

After you've identified the competencies needed for potential candidates in your succession plan, search online for relevant sources of training that you can recommend to potential candidates. Online tools are an increasingly valuable source of learning.

Reinforcing Your Competency Culture

The more effort you put into creating a competency culture, the easier it will be for you to identify and develop candidates to meet the needs of your succession plan. When every employee knows the importance of and is focused developing the competencies needed for his or her current position, as well as positions that will need to be filled in the future, your organization is far more likely to have available qualified candidates to meet the needs of your succession plan.

One very helpful strategy that reinforces a competency culture is to involve people throughout the organization in defining the competencies that are needed for the organization to achieve its mission. All too often, organizations create lofty mission statements, post them on their websites, hang copies on office walls, and print them on the backs of business cards. After a time, employees hardly notice them. These organizations miss a wonderful opportunity to focus everyone on the competencies needed to maximize the success of the organization.

Breathe life into your mission statement by involving every employee in a process of translating it into specific competencies that can be observed and/or measured:

1. **Meet with your managers and work with them to develop a list of specific behaviors that they'll strive to demonstrate on a daily basis in order to help the organization fulfill its mission.**

   Encourage managers to list those behaviors as personal commitments, making sure that they're specific and measurable.

2. **Ask the managers to meet with their employees and share these commitments with them.**

   The idea is for the managers to show their employees how the mission statement actually defines the competencies that the employees need to develop and demonstrate on the job.

3. **Ask managers to facilitate a group meeting with their employees to create a list of specific behaviors that illustrate the competencies they need to develop in order to play their part in achieving the organizational mission.**

4. **Have each manager and employee record his or her commitments, put them in a frame, and hang it next to a framed copy of the organizational mission statement.**

This process takes some time and effort to complete. But it's well worth that investment because it focuses everyone on the importance of defining and demonstrating needed competencies, which has several side-benefits for your organization:

✔ It creates an awareness of the interdependence of every person in achieving the organizational mission, which, in turn, reinforces a climate of teamwork.

✔ It provides you with additional standards for evaluating employee performance at every level of the organization.

✔ It will make it easier for you to identify people within your organization who are current or potential candidates for key positions.

Here are a few more ways to reinforce a competency culture in your organization:

✔ Help employees at all levels of the organization develop competency-based, individual development plans.

✔ Establish ongoing processes for identifying and developing internal successors, including the various assessments and observations described earlier. This will make it much easier for you in the future.

✔ Periodically, bring in trainers and professional speakers who focus on topics associated with competency development.

✔ Encourage managers to meet individually and on a group basis with their employees to provide special recognition to selected individuals who've been particularly successful in building their competencies.

Reinforcing your competency culture will make it much easier for you to implement a successful succession plan:

✔ Employees will have the needed knowledge and skills to contribute to the organization's long-term success, and they'll clearly understand their roles and the contributions they're expected to make.

✔ Employees will be more highly motivated to perform high-quality work, collaborate with others, and provide outstanding services to their customers.

✔ Employees will strive to do their best for themselves, for their teams, for the organization, and for customers. They'll do so because it's rewarding and satisfying to work extra hard in a competency culture.

✔ As a result of the increased levels of satisfaction, you're likely to find a decrease in employee absenteeism and turnover.

✔ Instead of blaming others for mistakes or making excuses, employees who want to improve their competencies will focus on using mistakes as opportunities to learn.

✔ With a focus on competencies, employees will be more productive.

Chapter 11

Aiming for a Smooth Transition

In This Chapter

▶ Helping new hires settle in

▶ Getting specific transition advice for your type of organization

▶ Handling office politics

*F*inding a successor to fill a position in your organization is hard work. But the fact that you've found the right person for the job doesn't guarantee that the transition will be a smooth one. Smooth transitions don't happen unless they're carefully planned, organized, and implemented.

So, what does a smooth transition look like? In a smooth transition,

✔ People are confident that nothing will change for the worse, and that business will go on as usual or even improve.

✔ People see that no important talents have been lost.

✔ The knowledge accumulated by the person leaving the organization isn't lost when that person walks out the door.

✔ People feel comfortable with the successor.

Aiming for a smooth transition. That's what this chapter is all about.

Making a New Hire Feel at Home

 Your successor may be someone promoted from within — and if so, you can skip this section. If your successor is a new hire, this section is for you. Here are some ways you can help a new hire feel at home in your organization, whether it's a major corporation or a small business:

✔ Familiarize the successor with his or her new office and introduce the successor to his or her new colleagues.

✔ Give the successor a tour of other offices and people with whom he or she will interact.

✔ Familiarize the successor with the available equipment, such as the phone system, computers, copiers, and fax machines.

✔ Provide the successor with any company-specific training, such as the use of company-specific software, special computer passwords, and so on.

✔ Give the successor a complete orientation that covers the full gamut of benefits (including vacation accrual, holidays, health insurance, pay periods, bonuses, confidentiality agreements, travel policy, and the like).

✔ If your organization has an employee handbook, provide it and have the successor sign a form indicating that he or she has received the handbook and agrees to abide by its contents.

✔ If possible, give the successor a way to get in touch with the person he or she replaced in case additional information is required.

✔ Assign someone as a resource person for the successor — someone he or she can call for the kinds of questions that come up when you're in a new environment and you don't know anyone.

Handling Successions in Specific Types of Organizations

Different kinds of organizations present different challenges to succession planning. So, it makes sense that the steps involved in a transition will vary from one type of organization to another.

In this section, I offer transition tips for all kinds of organizations — from large corporations to mom-and-pop businesses, from government organizations to educational institutions. No matter what kind of organization yours is, you'll find advice here on how to make a successor's transition problem-free.

Large for-profit organizations

Whether they provide products or services, for-profit organizations are in business to make money and share it with the organization's stakeholders. Generally, a for-profit organization is the result of several investors contributing financial resources and retaining key personnel to form a corporation. This typically includes a talented CEO and board of directors who may be given shares of stock or stock options in the corporation and who are appointed for fixed terms.

You can take some specific steps to make the transition of the CEO a smooth one. To aim for a smooth transition of a new CEO, keep the following tips in mind:

✔ **Coach the outgoing CEO on how to deal effectively with the transition of a successor into his or her position.** The more positively the outgoing CEO demonstrates active support for the experience, knowledge, skills, and abilities of the new CEO, the lower the anxiety, apprehension, and resistance of the employees.

You can start doing this before you've even found a successor for the departing CEO.

✔ **Before the new CEO's first day, make sure he or she is in sync with (or at least capable of adapting to) your organizational culture.** Every organization has its own set of norms, its own personality, and its own business processes. To help avoid a disruption in operations or anxiety among employees, your new CEO needs to meld into your organizational culture. This can be determined during the selection process (when you interview candidates through a series of open-ended questions directed at the candidate's managerial style) and by observing the candidate as he or she interacts with people in the organization.

✔ **Prepare a briefing book for the new CEO.** The briefing book should include a brief history of the organization, its financials, its strategic plan, its structure, its core strategies and capabilities, its array of products and/or services, and up-to-date bios of managers and people in other key positions.

✔ **Allow at least 90 days for the transition to take place.** During this transition period, the following steps should be taken if the departing CEO is available:

  • Have the departing CEO mentor the new CEO and familiarize him or her with the ins and outs of your organization and its financial structure, operations, and current challenges and opportunities.

  • Hold a series of orientation meetings with key groups in your organization in which the outgoing CEO and incoming CEO discuss the current and future states of the organization, with an emphasis on long-term performance. These meetings will help people feel comfortable with the change. If the departing CEO isn't available for these sessions, the new CEO should conduct them on his or her own.

- Use the transition period as an opportunity for knowledge transfer by having the departing CEO share with the new CEO the valuable knowledge accumulated during his or her tenure. This knowledge — about such things as important customer relationships, high CEO dependency on key people in the organization, operational problems that faced the departing CEO, and so on — will be immeasurably helpful to the new CEO in making a smooth transition.

- Encourage the departing CEO to share with the new CEO experiences he or she has had with board members, other key stakeholders, competitors, important customers, and people within your organization. Those experiences will give the new CEO guidelines for how to interact effectively with those constituencies.

As key stakeholders and shareholders in the organization, board members need to be fully involved with and publicly supportive of the new CEO. To aim for a smooth transition of a new CEO, engage the board in the following ways:

✔ Involve the board in developing a list of key organizational stakeholders that will be helpful for the new CEO to know.

✔ Have the board write a detailed letter about the incoming CEO for distribution to all shareholders and stakeholders. In that letter, have them include a description of the new CEO's background, along with an expression of enthusiastic support for him or her.

✔ Ask the board to prepare a news release announcing the hiring of the new CEO and distribute it to local newspapers, vendors, business publications, related business associations, and any other groups important to the organization. If the organization uses the services of a financial public relations firm, they should be involved in writing or at least reviewing this announcement.

✔ Have the departing CEO introduce the new CEO at a shareholder meeting, giving him or her visibly strong support.

Nonprofit organizations

Nonprofit organizations, such as charitable organizations, depend primarily on fundraising to survive. Like for-profit organizations, nonprofit organizations must generate revenue to pay bills and acquire assets. After doing so, however, they're different in the way they handle leftover money:

- For-profit organizations distribute leftover money among their shareholders and stakeholders.

- Nonprofit organizations, usually formed to help people by providing them with needed goods and/or services, use the leftover money to provide those goods or services and to strengthen the organization's infrastructure.

The founders of nonprofit organizations tend to be very passionate about what they do for the groups they serve. They have a clear vision of where they want the organization to go. Their passion inspires the people who work in the organization, as well as many others who volunteer their services or contribute funds for the organizational cause. In fact, it's that passion that often drives and defines the organizational culture.

When the time comes for founders to leave this type of organization, these personal characteristics can help or hinder a smooth transition.

On the helpful side, the passion should be a very visible piece of the transition process:

- During the transition, publicly emphasize the successor's passionate commitment to carrying on the mission of the organization, evidenced in part by his or her distinguished track record.

- Issue a special bulletin or some other form of communication in which you emphasize the impact your organization has had, and how the leadership transition is an exciting step toward even greater accomplishments. Distribute it to donors, grantees, and members of the community that your organization serves.

- Schedule meetings in which the founder, accompanied by the successor, meets with groups of employees and volunteers and speaks enthusiastically about the successor, reassuring everyone that the organization will continue to move forward in achieving the mission with no loss of energy, focus, passion, or commitment.

On the other hand, the founder's passion can get in the way of a smooth transition. In some cases, the powerful personality of founder leads to a lack of organizational decision making. Decisions are not made collectively, because the founder has seized control and won't relinquish it. This is known as the *founder's syndrome*. Here's how you can combat it to ensure a smooth transition:

> ✔ Prepare the founder early for an eventual transition. Hire a coach to help the founder spread his or her passion by developing a sound decision-making infrastructure in which collective decisions are made.
>
> You may have trouble convincing the founder to do this, but this step is critical. Without it, the organization's lack of capacity for shared decision making may hurt its performance during and after the transition.
>
> ✔ Involve the staff in developing a clear working credo that encourages all the stakeholders to engage in specific behaviors that help the organization continue to fulfill its mission, uninterrupted by a leadership transition. (See Chapter 10 for more information.)

Over time, the founders of nonprofit organizations generally develop relationships with donors, grantees, and members of the community. Successors have to do the same. Initially, founders should introduce successors to the people with whom they've developed relationships.

Before a founder physically leaves an organization, he or she should be given the opportunity to make a "grand exit." This means scheduling a public meeting to introduce the successor. The successor says very little other than acknowledging the introduction. The main thrust of the meeting is the founder reflecting on his or her time with the organization, lessons learned, and dreams of the future. This meeting is an opportunity for the founder to make a clean break with the organization, while at the same time championing the successor.

Small businesses

Small family-owned businesses and partnerships have their own special considerations when you're aiming for a smooth transition. Although there are differences in succession planning that depend on the size of the small business and the industry or profession in which it operates, take a moment to look at some suggestions that fit any small business. Whether a family-owned insurance agency, property management company, or apparel shop, they all share a few general considerations.

If the transition involves a new chief operating officer or owner of the business, keep the following tips in mind:

> ✔ Take the time before the transition to make sure that the corporate charter, by-laws, and stock certificates (if any) are up to date to avoid any confusion or problems for the successor.

✔ Clearly document that the successor will be personally protected from any litigation and claims that may be made against the organization for actions prior to his or her tenure. The successor needs to be free and clear of any threats.

✔ Prior to the transition, perform a complete review of business operations, including the identification of any problem areas. Clearly communicate to successors any problems that are in the pipeline in order to avoid surprises when the successor starts to work in the new job.

✔ Prior to the transition, prepare a complete inventory of current financial and accounting records, including outstanding payables and receivables, banking investment accounts, lists of creditors, loans from financial institutions or other investors, outstanding tax claims or IRS actions, and so on. One of the most damaging disruptions to a smooth transition is for the successor to be surprised by unexpected financial problems.

If the transition involves another key person in the business, keep the following tips in mind:

✔ In a small business, keeping all employees informed is particularly important. Their jobs depend on the performance of key people in the business. To avoid any drop in performance due to anxiety, make sure you provide employees with information regarding the transition process and the successor. Reassure people that the skills and qualifications of the successor will enable the organization to carry on business as usual, or even better. Getting out front with the information also helps prevent the rumor mill from controlling the story.

✔ Send out formal communication and publish legal notices about the transition so that interested parties such as competitors, customers, vendors, suppliers, and contractors will know what is happening with your business. Make sure that the notice includes a contact within the organization in case any of these parties have any questions.

In addition to these general considerations, there are some specific considerations that directly apply to family-owned businesses. (Although some family-owned businesses are large corporations, this section is directed at smaller family-owned businesses, which present their own challenges when aiming for a smooth transition.) Family hierarchies, family discord, disagreements about distribution of assets, IRS regulations, and tax liability issues all must be considered when a transition takes place.

Several steps should be taken by the family in advance of the owner's departure to set the stage for a smooth transition:

- ✔ Plan ahead and have all the details worked out long before there is any talk of retirement or unexpected departures.

- ✔ Family members need to meet and agree to a set of principles about how they want to see the business operate in the future. This should include a mission statement, a planned strategy for achieving the mission, and a description of the kind of organizational culture desired. This will make it easier for families to identify the right candidates when it comes to finding a qualified successor.

- ✔ Family members need to decide who in the family will be in the business in the long run and who will not.

- ✔ Similarly, family members must arrive at and agree to the results of an objective assessment of the competencies of family members to run the business. The owner's child may end up inheriting the family business, but that doesn't mean he or she has the competencies to run it.

- ✔ Establish a will, estate plan, buy/sell agreements, and shareholder agreements (if applicable). Have it all completed before the position change takes place in order to avoid any disruptions in a smooth transition.

Taking these steps typically requires the use of outside professionals. This is particularly true in a family characterized by a strong paternal hierarchy. In all cases, it's a good idea to seek counsel from an outside CPA and attorney, both of whom have expertise in business transitions, as well as a professional coach who can tactfully and expertly help the family arrive at decisions.

The main point is that if you're in a family-owned business, particularly if you're the founder of that business, you need to carefully plan any transitions in advance. It isn't only the founder's position that's critical. Family-owned businesses are most often small businesses. As a result, any and all positions are important.

Educational institutions

Succession planning in universities and colleges tends to focus primarily on leadership positions, such as department heads, deans, and chancellors and/or presidents.

Keep in mind three important characteristics of educational institutions when aiming for smooth transitions:

- ✔ **Many more constituencies are involved in college and universities, such as trustees, administrators, donors, alumni, and students.** A smooth transition is more likely to occur if the succession-planning process involves representatives of all the major constituencies. This will ensure more support for the successor during and after the transition.

✔ **Colleges and universities have a more collegial and democratic culture than a typical corporation.** Because a democratic culture often results in slower decision making, the institution must allow ample preplanning time to increase the likelihood that everyone involved is satisfied with the process, as well as the choice.

✔ **Colleges and universities have a system of shared government, including the president, the faculty, the non-faculty staff, and students.** It's very important, especially at higher levels of leadership, to make sure that all constituencies have been informed in advance.

If the successor is not a current employee of the institution, make sure that representatives of all constituencies are given an opportunity to meet with him or her. Invite the successor to present himself or herself at trustee meetings, meetings with other administrators, alumni meetings, donor meetings, and student association meetings.

The typical track for an academic leader follows a set progression from being a tenured faculty member, who is promoted to a full professor, to department chair, to a dean, and then to a chief academic officer. As a result, a successor is already known to most of the school's constituencies. The transition of an unknown, external successor to a leadership position can be very anxiety provoking and, as a result, requires extra time, communication, and involvement of all the key stakeholders.

Governmental organizations

Public agencies rarely undertake succession planning for a number of reasons, many of which are political. Government employees who were elected or appointed have time-defined tenure limitations. Often, they also have political ties to the administration that appointed them, so they assume that succession issues are not part of their job. Although this situation is slowly changing, it's still a slow process.

Here are some suggestions to facilitate the transition in a government organization:

✔ Keep the staff fully informed of the transition about to take place and make sure that everyone is knowledgeable about the successor.

- ✔ Higher leadership in a government department should be visibly involved in the transition process by supporting it and attending staff meetings to discuss it.

- ✔ The successor should review the key department initiatives already in place and work with the existing leadership team to continue or refine these initiatives as needed. A smooth transition is more likely to occur when the successor fully understands the department strategy already underway, and makes changes and adjustments only after careful deliberation and input from the key members of his or her leadership team.

- ✔ Make sure you schedule the successor to participate in meetings and discussions with his or her staff before assuming leadership responsibilities. In this way, the successor will be better prepared to take on the new position.

- ✔ Continue to use formal and informal communication channels to make sure that successors have a clear understanding of agency and departmental goals, processes, and operations.

The military is a special case of a government organization. Succession planning has been a military tradition for over 200 years. The military identifies leaders far in advance and continuously develops them while bringing them up through the ranks. However, the goal of leaders in both nonmilitary and military governmental organizations is the same: to work hard at mobilizing people to accomplish strategic missions. Smoother transitions occur when you take the steps described in this section to make sure that successors are fully informed, committed, and prepared to assume key leadership roles.

Dealing with Internal Dynamics

Organizations are groups of people, and all groups of people are blessed (or cursed) with internal dynamics — power struggles, gossip, competition. Every organization develops its own organizational culture, its own formal and informal set of do's and don'ts, cliques, rumormongers, and favorites.

When a new person moves into a vacated position, especially if he or she is an external candidate, some of these internal dynamics likely will interfere with a smooth transition. The key is to recognize and deal with your organization's internal dynamics long before a transition, and throughout the transition process.

In this section, I offer several strategies for dealing with internal dynamics.

Helping managers develop an empowering culture

Begin by training managers and supervisors how to develop an *empowering* organizational climate in which people feel a strong sense of ownership of their work. Employees who own and feel in control of their work believe managers trust them, and this sense of trust has a measurably positive impact on motivation, morale, and productivity.

Here are some things you can do to foster an empowering culture:

✓ **Move managerial thinking away from disciplining and toward coaching.** Train managers to be facilitators or catalysts who help employees develop their skills and unleash their talents.

✓ **Train managers to support and reinforce their employees, continuously encouraging them to bring out their best.**

✓ **Create an organizational atmosphere of continuous learning and collaborative problem solving.** This will help move all the employees into alignment with your organization's mission.

✓ **Keep employees informed about changes and developments in the organization.** This transparency will help the employees feel more secure in their jobs, better about their work, more respected, and more confident in their managers and top management.

When mangers focus on bringing out the best in every employee, instead of commanding and directing them, they'll create a feeling of empowerment among employees. And when employees feel empowered, they're likely to trust management in making transition decisions.

Creating a problem-solving mindset

Actively involve employees in the improvement of existing organizational processes and the development of new ones, in order to create a problem-solving mindset. Start by training people throughout the organization in process improvement methodologies and tools.

Form temporary teams to tweak processes — teams that are explicitly formed to strike quickly to improve a specific process. Start by training people throughout the organization in process improvement methodologies and tools to prepare them to participate in the temporary teams when a process improvement need arises.

Encourage everyone to participate in these temporary teams. This will stimulate a problem-solving mindset throughout your organization, while reducing the tendency to point fingers and blame others. Reward successful teams with special incentives, such as gift cards for dinners or ones they can use to shop at local stores.

Taking all these steps to create a problem-solving mindset will help develop a cooperative, empowering organizational climate in which people will feel more ownership of their work and more accepting of whatever changes are made by management, including transition decisions.

Promoting teamwork

You want to think of your organization as one whole entity, as opposed to lots of separate departments or individual people. You can use the following techniques to promote a view of organization-wide interdependency in achieving your organizational mission:

- ✔ **Publish periodic newsletters (online or hard copy) to build a sense of shared connectedness.** Share important events, such as birthdays, awards, and any other news that highlights employees. For each issue, interview people in a different section of your organization. Write an article about them. People in other sections will learn about them and develop a stronger sense of camaraderie and collaboration.

- ✔ **Involve employees in experiences that promote teamwork.** This could range from elaborate activities, such as weekend team-building retreats, to simple, everyday activities, such as bringing a favorite dessert to the employee lunch room to share with everyone.

- ✔ **Conduct organization-wide training focused on how to improve communication and cooperation.** You can bring in a consultant to lead the session, or work with HR to develop this kind of training.

- ✔ **Hold interdepartmental problem-solving sessions.** Bring together employees from different parts of the organization to discuss their working relationship and the ways in which they can help each other perform more effectively.

When you implement strategies such as these, people will see and appreciate what other people are contributing to the organization's success. This will highlight their sense of interdependence and strengthen their ability to work together as one organization-wide team. It also will help minimize the negative effects of internal dynamics on transition decisions.

Building a climate of trust

One of the most effective ways to ensure a smooth transition of a successor, particularly when it comes to a key leadership position, is to build an organizational climate of trust well before the transition takes place. The more employees trust one another, their managers, and the leaders of the organization, the more accepting they'll be of any transitions involving key positions.

Managers play a critical role in building a climate of trust. The following sections offer trust-building tips for you and your managers.

Helping people feel they belong

Most employees want to feel like they're part of a family at work. After all, many of them spend more time at work than they do at home with their own families. They want to be with people who care about each other and have a shared sense of priorities, values, and mutual expectations. In other words, they want to feel like they belong.

Here's how to help people feel at home:

✔ **Cultivate a family climate.** Encourage everyone to make the effort to know something about their co-workers. A cheery "good morning." A question or two here and there about how someone is doing. An inquiry about the state of a sick child. All this helps employees feel they're part of a group that cares, which reinforces a family feeling in the organization.

✔ **Acknowledge the key events of others.** If someone has a death in the family, a child getting married, a new grandchild, a graduation, or a significant birthday, encourage people to acknowledge the event. A kind, sympathetic, caring, or congratulatory word or action goes a long way toward making people feel they're part of a family culture at work.

✔ **Help others with their work when they're overwhelmed.** Don't let people fall into the trap of "That's not *my* job!" It's the job of everyone to make sure that things get done in pursuit of the organizational mission. In those times when individual workloads become very heavy and hard to manage, encourage employees to pitch in and help out, even if it isn't in their job descriptions. And be sure to recognize them when they do so.

Helping people feel they belong builds bonds of trust. A climate of trust enhances your chances of a smooth transition.

Promoting mutual respect

Strong relationships are built on mutual respect. Mutual respect means that people regard each other with esteem and accept each other for who they are. Essentially, this means treating each other honestly, openly, and as adults. The more that people demonstrate respect for their fellow employees, the more they'll appreciate and trust one another.

With that in mind, educate your managers to do the following:

✓ **Communicate with others from a "win/win" position.** This means communicating with other people in ways that convey to them that they, just like you, have their own unique sets of talents and skills. You may know how to effectively manage, but your best IT person may know how to fix a software problem. When you communicate with others on this kind of equal plane, you signal to them that you respect them. By doing so, you increase the likelihood that they'll respect you.

✓ **Actively listen to others when they express themselves.** Not paying attention to what someone is telling you is a signal of disrespect. Continually practice the principles of active listening:

  • Don't talk over them.

  • Stay focused.

  • Don't allow interruptions.

Listen objectively and analytically. Pay attention to their nonverbal behaviors that tell you how they really feel, even if they don't talk about it. In order to demonstrate your interest, as well as increase your comprehension, rephrase the comments that are expressed to you and ask if your interpretation is correct. Guard against reacting critically because someone pushed one of your emotional buttons.

✓ **Acknowledge the contributions of others.** When someone has an idea, don't immediately point out flaws in his thinking or describe a better idea you have. Listen to him to understand his point of view. Don't simply overrun his suggestion with an idea of your own. If you do believe you can improve on his idea or that you have a better one, be tactful in introducing your thinking. Say something like "That's an interesting idea. I see where you're going, and what if we tried . . . ?"

Win/win communication, active listening, and acknowledging the contributions people make will help build a climate of trust, which, in turn, will contribute to smooth transitions.

Recognizing a job well done

People want their managers and supervisors to recognize them when they do something well. In spite of all the talk these days about the decline of the work ethic, the truth is that most people are motivated to do a good job. However, they're less motivated and more distrustful of managers and supervisors who rarely pat them on the back and talk to them only when things go wrong.

Here are some ways that managers can recognize employees' contributions:

- ✔ **Praise employees for a job well done.** Managers are constantly under pressure, busy responding to multiple demands. As a result, many managers only comment to employees about their performance when things are going wrong, not when they're going right. Don't fall into that trap. Look for opportunities to praise. Make a daily habit of finding people to praise. Such feedback is motivational and improves employees' self-esteem, as well as their performance.

- ✔ **Coach supervisors to praise their employees.** Talk about praising employees in staff meetings. You may even ask the attendees to bring in actual examples of ways in which they've recognized their employees during the previous couple weeks. Including this type of discussion in regular staff meetings will help employees develop a habit of rewarding solid performance.

- ✔ **Encourage everyone to make a habit of praising others for work well done.** In meetings with your employees, urge them to compliment others when they see them doing something beyond the call of duty. Everyone likes a pat on the back!

When people know they're appreciated, they're less likely to feel threatened when a new person enters the scene.

Being responsive to employees

Here are some trust-building tips for you, your managers, and your supervisors to help them be more responsive to employees. Discuss these in meetings and encourage your entire team to take the following steps:

- ✔ **Honor commitments.** When you tell your employees that you'll do something, they expect you to do it. In particular, employees distrust managers or supervisors who don't follow through on commitments. How can they trust you if you never do what you say you're going to do? They want you to be reliable, dependable, and true to your word.

✔ **Reliably respond to suggestions.** As a manager or supervisor, when an employee offers a suggestion for improving a situation, implement it, explain why it can't be implemented, or promise to get back to him or her. If you tell employees you'll get back to them, be sure to do so promptly, even if it's to explain why a suggestion can't be implemented.

✔ **Don't make promises you can't keep.** Because some managers want to be the "good guy" with their employees, they rush to make promises before they really know if they can keep them. If you aren't sure you can keep a particular promise, the way to build trust is by telling the employees, "I'll check into it." Then you have to follow up by getting back to them with an answer.

Taking these steps will add another piece to the process of building a climate of trust, which is so important when you're aiming for a smooth transition.

Developing your own managerial competence

Employees respect competent managers and supervisors. Employees expect their leaders to be knowledgeable, not only in terms of managerial skills, but also in terms of expertise associated with the jobs they oversee. Employees are less likely to trust a manager or supervisor who doesn't know the jobs of his or her employees.

Here are some suggestions for developing the kind of managerial competences that will engender trust in your employees:

✔ **Encourage the managers in your organization to learn what their employees do if they don't already know.** Sometimes people rapidly rise through the ranks and become managers without detailed knowledge of what many of their employees do. If that's the case for some managers in your organization, encourage them to take the time to systematically learn what each of their employees does. Managers who understand their employees' jobs, roles, and functions tend to generate high levels of trust.

✔ **Encourage the managers in your organization to never fake it.** If managers don't know the ins and outs of an employee's job, advise them to avoid pretending that they do. At the same time, encourage these managers to take active and immediate steps to upgrade their knowledge and understanding of their employees' work. They can do so in a number of ways, such as by increased observation of their employees, directed readings, or formal classes. They can even mention to their employees that they'd like to learn from them, a request that virtually all employees are more than happy to oblige. By dealing honestly and openly with employees, especially in this type of situation, managers and employees are better able to strengthen the bonds of mutual respect and trust. When managers fake it, employees quickly spot the incompetence, and they react with distrust.

Letting employees work without being micromanaged

Some managers and supervisors insist that everything be done *their* way. They hover over their employees to make sure that work is done exactly as they want it. They don't know how or when to delegate responsibilities and then follow up as needed. They convey a belief that nobody can do the job as well as they can. One common outcome of this managerial practice is that employees end up feeling distrusted.

You can counter this behavior by doing the following:

- ✔ **Encourage the managers in your organization to adjust their leadership style to fit the situation.** Depending upon the knowledge, skills, and abilities of their individual employees, along with such factors as time constraints, resources required, and financial impact of a given project, managers should opt for a leadership approach that best fits the overall situation. In some cases, tighter managerial direction will be required; other situations call for more of a hands-off approach in which the employees have more freedom, discretion, and autonomy. By relying on just one style, especially micromanagement, managers tend to increase dissatisfaction as well as distrust.

- ✔ **Make sure that managers in your organization are providing employees with the information they need to do a great job.** Whether the employees are working on projects that offer a high degree of autonomy or projects that require closer monitoring, employees should be kept informed. When communication is clear and direct, not only are employees able to do a better job (because they fully understand what's being asked of them), but also their performance is enhanced by the clear message of trust and respect that is implicitly conveyed. This is the exact opposite of the message that is conveyed by micromanaging.

Part IV
Keeping the Succession Ball Rolling

The 5th Wave — By Rich Tennant

"Another successful transfer of power."

In this part . . .

This part demonstrates the key roles of open and ongoing communication and support in every aspect of your succession plan, from creation to implementation. Communication and support are particularly important in the rapidly changing workplaces of the 21st century. Technology, social media, generational differences, and the Internet all combine to keep today's organizations in a steady state of flux. It's in this ever-changing context that succession planning must take root and flourish. By providing support to the existing members of your organization, as well as to new hires, you'll be able to build continuity and strengthen your organization's ability to deal with the unexpected.

This part provides you with an understanding of the widespread changes in today's organizations, as well as the ways in which your succession plan can build on these changes, instead of being sidetracked by them.

Chapter 12

Making Great Exits

In This Chapter
▶ Taking actions before, during, and after an exit
▶ Anticipating and preparing for challenges

A key part of any succession plan isn't just finding a successor for the person who's leaving, but making sure that the exit itself is a good one. Making a great exit is essential. The secret is being prepared and following through.

In this chapter, I tell you what you can do to ensure the great exits of key personnel.

Not only will these steps help you accomplish great exits, but they can actually create a positive atmosphere of anticipation among your employees, a spirit of renewal and growth.

Before the Exit

The best way to ensure a great exit is to make sure that your succession plan has the full support of your organization — from the CEO and board of directors on down. You can lay the foundation for a great exit by getting this support well before the exit occurs.

So, what kind of support do you need and where do you start? That's what I cover in this section.

Enlisting the support of your managers

Managers play an important role in shaping the organizational climate. They're responsible for getting work done. And while they're getting work done, their managerial styles, personalities, and behaviors directly influence how well employees perform and feel about their jobs. Employee morale and the degree of employee trust in the organization's future are profoundly influenced by managers.

So, how do you go about enlisting the support of managers and helping them create a climate of acceptance and trust for the new hire? Here are some tips:

- ✔ **Get managers' input during the planning process.** The more managers feel some ownership of your plan, the more likely they'll be to support it and facilitate it.

- ✔ **Get managers' help in defining needed competencies.** Managers have lots of hands-on experiences with talented people, from CEOs to talent in other key positions. They often know what kind of person works and what kind of person doesn't, and why. Tap into their experience.

- ✔ **Ask managers to help identify external talent sources.** Managers talk to other managers in other organizations at conferences, workshops, and the like. They develop an awareness of where good people can be found. Tap into that awareness.

- ✔ **Ask managers for help in identifying internal talent sources.** Managers observe promising talent in their own departments. Depending on the size and culture of an organization, they often see talent in other areas of the organization as well. Tap into their perceptiveness.

- ✔ **Keep managers informed about the progress of your succession plan throughout the planning process.** Keep them up to date about how the succession-planning process is developing and its importance to and impact on the organization. Discuss major changes with them and consider any input they may offer.

The more invested managers feel in your succession plan, the more help they'll be in making any exit a great one by reinforcing its positive effects on the organization.

Getting the support of your board

Many organizations, particularly larger ones, have boards of directors. Their responsibilities vary from simply being advisory (usually in smaller organizations) to governing (typically in larger organizations).

Whichever role the board plays, its primary job over the long run is to help ensure that the organization fulfills its mission statement. Given that responsibility, if you have a board of directors, all the board members must fully support your succession plan.

The board's support is especially critical when it's the CEO or someone else in upper management who's exiting, because those departures generally have a more widespread impact on the organizational climate.

You can get the support of your board in a few key ways:

✔ **Involve them in the planning process.** Like day-to-day managers, board members will be more committed to and more likely to offer vocal support for your plan, if they're involved in its conceptualization. If they've played a role in designing the plan, they'll want to let people know they support it.

✔ **Get board members to spend time with selected new hires.** This step is especially important when you're hiring a new CEO or key manager. The more board members get to know and feel comfortable with the new hire, the easier it will be for them to give visibly positive support for the exit taking place.

✔ **Make the board's support visible to everyone.** Often, employees know very little about the board beyond that it exists. But they know that the board is somehow important to the success of the organization. So, give your board members a stage. Quote their support in meetings, memos, articles, e-mails, and other forms of communication.

Learning from exiting personnel

Assuming the vacancy being filled isn't due to a death, that departing person can be a reservoir of valuable information and opinions that can immediately help the new hire and, in the long run, your organization. During the pre-exit phase, learn as much as you can from the person leaving.

Hold a face-to-face meeting with the exiting person, and ask the following questions:

✔ Where do you keep any files that will be used by or in some way helpful to the new hire?

✔ Is any useful electronic information stored on hard drives and memory devices? If so, where?

✔ Is there anything else you use to enrich your knowledge about the job and the organization and its functioning, such as annual reports, newspaper articles, and so on?

✔ Are there external contacts in other organizations, including professional associations, that will be useful to the new hire?

✔ Do you have valued customer contacts who can provide helpful suggestions for improving products and/or services?

✔ Which suppliers have been particularly helpful to you?

✔ When you think back, what has been the most frustrating, difficult, or upsetting thing that's happened to you in your work here?

✔ How do you feel about the organizational culture or climate?

✔ Do you have any suggestions for how communication could be improved in the organization?

✔ What policies do you think get in the way of good work in this organization? Do you have any suggestions for policy changes we could make?

✔ Do you have any suggestions on how working conditions could be improved in this organization?

✔ Do you think our equipment and machinery could be improved and if so, how?

✔ Do you have any suggestions for how customer service can be improved?

✔ How could the organization have helped you make fuller use of your talents, experience, and capabilities?

✔ What training, workshops, conferences, or other such events did you find most helpful in the performance of your job? Which ones were least useful?

✔ Is there any training that would've been helpful to you that you didn't get?

✔ Do you have any examples of things that get in the way of good work, such as time-wasting meetings, bureaucratic procedures, pointless reports, and so on?

✔ What do you think of communication, cooperation, and coordination between the departments? Are there any interdepartmental issues or problems that need further attention? If so, do you have any suggestions for dealing with them?

✔ What could have been changed or done differently to help you make more effective use of your time?

✔ Of the employees in your department, which ones show the greatest potential for growth and advancement?

✔ What has been the most enjoyable and satisfying thing for you about working here?

✔ Do you have any other suggestions that would help us make this a better organization?

Based on what you learn, meet with your key people to discuss what you could change or add to help the new hire meld into the organization. You also may use some of the departing employee's suggestions to get the new hire involved in improving organizational functioning.

Educating the new hire

Getting organizational support for an exit about to take place is only half the story. The other half is educating the selected new hires, even before they take their new positions. All too often, organizations don't give this part enough attention.

Here are several suggestions for readying the new hire to assume his or her position:

- ✔ **Familiarize the new hire with your organization.** Give the new hire a tour so he or she can get an impression of your organization's size, its structure, where it's located, and so on. In larger workplaces, a basic map that includes the location of the departments, restrooms, and emergency exits is a valuable tool.

- ✔ **Make sure he or she is familiar with your organization's strategic plan, its vision, and its mission.** Whether an upper manager or a key talent in some critical part of your organization, it's very important for the new hire to be completely aware of what your organization is doing, where it's going, and what it aspires to be. In addition to discussing these topics with a new hire, this type of information will be further reinforced if the company overview and mission statement are also available in written form, whether online or in hard copy.

- ✔ **Help the new hire learn even more about your organization.** Provide the new hire with any publications or data that will help him or her learn more details about your organization, such as newspaper articles or survey results from employee and customer surveys. If the company has received awards or recognition from associations or governmental agencies, such as for its success in customer service or sustainability, these accolades should also be shared with the new hire.

- ✔ **Introduce the new hire to the person being replaced.** Facilitate a meeting between them and a sharing of what goes into the job of the person exiting. This will provide the new hire with information critical to the performance of his or her new job. It also will signal to others in your organization that the exit is taking place smoothly and that life will go on as usual.

✔ **Invite the new hire to sit in on meetings involving the person he or she is replacing**. As an observer in those meetings, the new hire will learn more about the new position and your organization.

✔ **Have the new hire shadow the person being replaced for a period of time.** This step is especially important if the new person is at an upper-management level and is being hired from outside your organization, rather than being promoted from within. In some organizations, the new CEO shadows the CEO being replaced for as long as a year before assuming the position.

The more you educate your new hires about your organization in advance, the smoother the exits of the people they're replacing will be.

During the Exit

No matter how well planned, the exit of a key talent can be very disruptive in any organization when people throughout the organization don't really know what's going on. In this section, I cover specific steps you can take during the exit to make it a good one.

Keeping your managers informed

The role of managers continues to be important in the exit process as it's taking place. Keep your managers in the loop by doing the following:

✔ **Use all your available communication channels.** Inform managers about the plan's progress in regular management meetings, in periodic update memos, by e-mail, and so on.

✔ **Don't limit your informing them to succession planning at the top level.** In other words, don't only keep them informed when the succession plan involves an upper manager or a fellow manager. Inform them about other key position changes. The success of your organization likely depends on the performance of other key talent. Some organizations thrive because of innovative IT talent; others, because of outstanding salespeople.

✔ **Involve managers themselves in the informing process.** Encourage managers to share their awareness of the exit that is occurring with their employees, as well as with vendors and customers with whom they come into contact.

The more managers are informed, the more capable they'll be of painting a positive picture of a departure and helping make the exit a great one.

Keeping employees in the loop

Employees talk and rumors spread in the face of any major change. The exit of key talent often leads to people feeling anxious about their own jobs. Don't let that happen. Be alert for rumors, and counter them with accurate information when they occur.

Here's how to keep employees informed during an exit:

- ✔ **If your organization is small, include all employees in periodic organization-wide meetings.** Bring them up to speed on what's happening and what key personnel changes are likely to be taking place.

- ✔ **Do the same in departmental or section meetings, especially if your organization is too large to hold organization-wide meetings.** This will reinforce their knowledge about key personnel changes taking place.

- ✔ **Establish and use employee newsletters to keep people up to date on people leaving, when they'll be leaving, and who will be taking their place.**

- ✔ **Counter any rumors with clear-cut information.** You want to prevent employees from feeling demoralized and anxiety from spreading.

The more accurate the information employees have about a smooth transition, the more confident and relaxed they'll feel about their future in your organization, the more supportive they'll be of the changes that are implemented, and the greater the exit.

Helping a new hire feel welcomed

Facilitating the departure of key personnel is only half the story of a great exit. The other half is integrating new hires into the organization in a way that makes them feel right at home. Here are several suggestions for helping you do that:

- ✔ **Introduce the new hire to the department heads and other key people in the organization.** The more the new hire is integrated into the organization, the more he or she will feel connected to and part of it.

✔ **Introduce the new hire to his or her new colleagues in their work settings.** The more the new hire knows about and feels comfortable with his or her future associates at work, the more he or she will feel welcomed while assuming the job.

✔ **Encourage people to socialize with new hires over lunch or dinner, or in other social settings.** The more the new hire is connected to future associates, the more he or she will feel welcomed into the workplace.

Helping the new hire feel welcomed will contribute to making the exit of the person being replaced a great one.

After the Exit

Someone leaving and a new person taking his or her place doesn't mean the exit process is over. You can take steps to wrap up the exit successfully.

Supporting the new hire

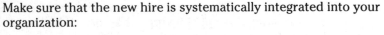

Make sure that the new hire is systematically integrated into your organization:

✔ Engage the new hire in a frank discussion about any concerns or worries he or she has about joining your organization.

✔ Offer your support in helping the new hire deal with those concerns and resolve any problems while adjusting to the new position.

✔ Provide the new hire with useful training that will help him or her ease into the new job, such as any acronyms, processes, or procedures that are unique to your organization.

✔ Make sure the new hire has the people and equipment he or she needs to comfortably ease into the job.

✔ Introduce the new hire to any vendors or key customers with whom he or she will be dealing on the job.

Revising the exit process where necessary

Some exits are great exits, smoothly unfolding without a hitch. Others run into unanticipated problems. Think about any problems that occur and come up with suggested revisions of the succession plan that would solve them.

Keep a log to record your observations of the entire exit process from start to finish. Record what you observe working well and what you see not working quite right, including the following:

- ✔ **Talent pools:** Did you tap the right talent pools?

- ✔ **Manager support for the plan:** Did you get the support of managers for the exit plan?

- ✔ **Board support for the plan:** Did you get the visible support of board members for the exit plan?

- ✔ **Employee support for the plan:** Did you get the support of employees for the exit plan?

- ✔ **Educating the new hire:** Were there any problems educating the new hire about your organization?

- ✔ **Informing managers:** Did you run into any problems keeping your managers informed?

- ✔ **Informing employees:** Were you able to successfully keep your employees in the loop?

- ✔ **Welcoming the new hire:** Did you run into any problems while helping the new hire feel welcomed to your organization?

- ✔ **Support for the new hire:** Were you able to provide sufficient support to the new hire, to help him or her ease into the new job?

Based on your log of observations about how well the exit process took place, take the following actions:

- ✔ Identify steps in the plan needing changing, and specify how you may change them.

- ✔ Consult with other people involved in the exit process in a search for additional observations and actions about the process.

- ✔ Construct a report of your findings for delivery to the succession-planning team.

- ✔ Meet with the succession-planning team to deliver the report and share your suggestions.

- ✔ Brainstorm with the succession-planning team to find solutions for problems that you weren't able to solve.

- ✔ Revise the plan with the team to help ensure a great exit for the next key personnel change.

Learn from the exit process. That will help you make the next exit even better!

Expecting the Unexpected

You've done it right. You set the stage for a great exit. You garnered all the support you needed. You kept everyone informed. You educated the new hire about your organization and made him or her feel welcome. You've done everything possible to create a great exit.

But then — oops! — something happens. An unexpected event occurs that undermines all your hard work. How you deal with that event will determine whether you can still produce a great exit.

In other words, be prepared for the unexpected, such as the situations I cover in this section.

Something happens to the new hire

The new hire may become too ill to take the job or even die. Suddenly, in the middle of it all, you're left with no candidate. What do you do?

- Make sure you have backup talent — other people you've interviewed who may still be available to fill the position.
- Immediately inform everyone and reassure them that you're handling it.
- Counter rumors quickly before they have a chance to spread and multiply.

Something happens to the economy

The economy crashes, falling into a deep, debilitating recession in the middle of the exit process, and consumer confidence plunges. Here's how to respond:

- Meet with your key people to immediately assess the impact of the recession on your organization and any resulting implications for your planned personnel change.
- Decide if you'll proceed or delay the new hire.
- If you decide to delay, determine how the functions of the now-empty position will be covered.

✔ Inform everyone of your decisions and reassure people that you're handling it.

✔ Again, counter rumors immediately, before they have a chance to spread and multiply.

Something happens in the marketplace

A competitor suddenly offers new and better versions of what you offer at a better price. Or a new technology emerges that outdates what you have and puts you at a major disadvantage. Here's what to do:

✔ Meet with your key people to determine if the candidate you're about to hire will have the competencies needed to deal with the changes.

✔ Decide if you'll proceed with hiring the candidate or look for new, more appropriate talent.

✔ Check your backup talent pool to see if other people you've interviewed may have the right competencies to help put you back in a competitive position.

✔ Inform everyone of your decisions, and reassure people that you're handling it.

✔ Counter rumors immediately, before they have a chance to spread and multiply.

Something in your perception of the new hire changes

In the process of educating and integrating the new hire, it suddenly becomes apparent to you that this person is not the kind of person or does not have the kind of competencies you were led to believe. Here's what to do:

✔ Always use a probationary period (for example, 90 days) to enable you change your mind about the new hire if necessary.

✔ If you haven't yet completed the exit process, stop it immediately.

✔ Inform everyone about what's happening, and reassure people that you'll be able to handle it.

- ✔ Counter rumors immediately, before they have a chance to spread and multiply.

- ✔ Check your backup talent pool to see if other people you've interviewed may be a better fit.

- ✔ Vet your new selection carefully before you proceed with the process.

Chapter 13

Maintaining Your Plan in Today's Changing Workplace

In This Chapter

▶ Understanding how generational and cultural diversity impact the workplace

▶ Seeing how changes in technology impact an organization

▶ Adjusting your succession plan to adapt to workplace trends

*I*n every generation, you hear people talking about how the world has changed. "Things aren't what they used to be!" "I don't understand this younger generation!" "People just don't have the kind of manners they used to have!" And so on. Which just goes to show you: If there is any single, unchanging constant in life, it's change itself.

But today's workplace is changing more rapidly and more dramatically than ever before. People are more connected at a global level, quickly sharing opinions, problems, promotions, news, and all kinds of other information. There is an interlocked network of financial institutions, and huge corporations are doing business all around the world. A growing volume of production and services are being outsourced to companies in developing countries. An increasingly diverse workforce has been made possible by more accessible global travel and relocation. Older workers are working longer due to a combination of longer life spans, advances in the health field, and economic necessity.

All these trends have significant implications for succession planning. And that's what this chapter is all about.

In order to adjust your succession plan to the trends in today's workplace, you need to fully understand those trends. Consequently, a good portion of this chapter is devoted to providing you with that understanding. I also offer suggestions for adapting your succession plan.

The knowledge you gain in understanding these trends will not only help you adjust your succession plan, but provide you with a broader look at steps you can take to create a workplace that's actively supportive of succession planning.

Three Key Trends in Today's Workplace

Three important threads run through today's changing workplace:

- ✔ A greater mixture of generations than ever before
- ✔ An increase in cultural diversity in both global and non-global organizations
- ✔ A dramatic technological explosion, generating computer and social-media tools of all kinds

These trends are significantly affecting personnel needs and job performance at every organizational level. They call for new competencies, new ways of doing things, and more flexible management styles, all of which have implications for your developing and maintaining an effective succession plan.

However, in order for you to gain a complete understanding of how these factors will influence your succession-planning process, you need to be familiar with the characteristics of each. You find the information you need in this section.

The multigenerational workplace

If your organization is large (and you've been in the workforce a while), you've probably noticed a greater mixture of generations in recent years than you saw in the past. Four very different generations are present in today's workplace:

- ✔ **Veterans (also known as Traditionalists):** People born between 1922 and 1945
- ✔ **Baby Boomers:** People born between 1946 and 1964
- ✔ **Generation Xers:** People born between 1965 and 1980
- ✔ **Millennials (also known as Generation Yers or Nexters):** People born between 1981 and 2000

Each generation has its own set of core values, personal attributes, expectations at work, and work habits.

Core values

Each generation, influenced by the particular events dominating its time, developed its own unique set of core values.

These differences in values affect how the generations perform in the workplace, which has direct relevance to the processes you develop for selecting candidates in your succession planning.

Veterans

Veterans came of age during the Great Depression and World War II, a time of military structure and orderliness. They value

- ✔ Conformity
- ✔ Discipline
- ✔ Authority
- ✔ Obedience
- ✔ Duty before pleasure
- ✔ Law and order
- ✔ Patriotism

Baby Boomers

Baby Boomers, born during or after World War II, grew up during a time of economic growth and expansion. They value

- ✔ Optimism
- ✔ New opportunities
- ✔ Progress
- ✔ Equal opportunities for everyone
- ✔ Equal rights

Generation Xers

Generation Xers grew up in a time when working mothers were more common and education was emphasized. They value

- ✔ Learning
- ✔ Informality
- ✔ Fun
- ✔ Independence
- ✔ Self-reliance
- ✔ Skepticism

Millennials

Millennials grew up in an era in which parents pampered children and emphasized a focus on every aspect of life, such as getting good grades, playing a musical instrument, and participating in sports. They value

- ✔ Confidence
- ✔ Independence
- ✔ Community
- ✔ Collaboration
- ✔ Tolerance
- ✔ Diversity
- ✔ Creativity

Personal attributes

As a result of the times in which they grew up and the core values that emerged from their experiences, the different generations are typified by slightly different clusters of personal attributes.

These personal attributes have significant implications for how people will perform at work and, consequently, how you'll develop and maintain your succession plan.

Veterans

Veterans hold more traditional values and are more structured in their approach to work. Veterans

- ✔ Are competent, conservative, ethical, dedicated, organized, and task oriented
- ✔ View education as a dream and have fewer higher-education degrees than other generations
- ✔ Are fiscally prudent and comfortable with doing more with less
- ✔ Have developed their competencies over time by working hard at their jobs, and typically are near the end of a lifelong career with one organization

Baby Boomers

Baby Boomers are motivated to demonstrate their abilities. Baby Boomers

- ✔ Are ambitious, competitive, idealistic, and willing to take on responsibility

✔ Are competent at their work and have the ability to handle crises

✔ Have good communication skills and prefer consensus leadership

✔ View education as a birthright

✔ Look for development opportunities beyond formal education at work in the form of training, coaching, and/or mentoring

Generation Xers

Generation Xers are more skeptical than other generations. Generation Xers

✔ Are confident, competent, creative, and independent

✔ Are self-starters, willing to take on responsibility and willing to put in extra time to get a job done

✔ Are pragmatic and results driven

✔ Will question a particular task if they can't see the reason for it

✔ See education as a way to get where they want to go

✔ Are technologically savvy, having learned how to use computers in elementary school

Millennials

Millennials are more focused on what they want at work. Millennials

✔ Are ambitious and very independent

✔ Love to collaborate and are at ease in teamwork, even though they're very individualistic

✔ Respect competencies not titles

✔ Are community minded and want to make contributions to the world

✔ Are comfortable with diversity

✔ Are globally oriented and the best educated of all generations

✔ Are motivated to learn

✔ Are the most technically sophisticated of all generations, having grown up with a variety of new social media

Expectations at work

Accompanying the value differences among generations are differences in their expectations of others at work.

Expectations are critically important in everyone's life. When expectations are met, people are happy. When expectations are not met, people are disappointed and possibly even disillusioned. Your succession plan should include a process for uncovering the expectations of any successor candidates.

Veterans

Veterans expect

- Recognition and respect for their experience
- Everyone to respect authority, follow the rules, and obey orders
- People to be dedicated and willing to make sacrifices
- Their organization to have a good reputation and to be ethical in its dealings with employees, customers, and any other groups with which it interacts

Baby Boomers

Baby Boomers expect

- To be personally gratified by their work
- Personal attention, recognition, and promotion
- That their experience will be valued
- To receive credit and be respected for their accomplishments
- Clear and concise job descriptions
- That they will see work as an exciting adventure

Generation Xers

Generation Xers expect

- To have a family feeling at work
- Informality and casual-dress days
- To have fun at work
- Flexibility in scheduling projects and work hours
- Their performance to be evaluated on how well it's done and not on other factors (such as favoritism, age, or seniority)

Millennials

Millennials expect

- To work with positive people and an organization that can help them fulfill their dreams

✔ To be challenged by their work (they're easily bored)

✔ That they will gain new knowledge and skills in their jobs

✔ To be well paid

Work behaviors

Generational differences in values, personal attributes, and expectations lead to differences in work behaviors.

You have to take into account these differences in work behaviors when hiring a successor for any position. They'll determine how well a successor performs on the job and melds with the organization.

Veterans

Veterans in the workplace

✔ See work as an obligation

✔ Believe people should work before having fun

✔ Are hard workers

✔ Are usually loyal to their employers

✔ Believe in sticking to the rules

✔ Tend to see organizations as a hierarchy and lead in a command-and-control style when they hold leadership positions

✔ See a clear separation between their work and family lives

Baby Boomers

Baby Boomers in the workplace

✔ Are workaholics, deriving their personal fulfillment from their work

✔ Question authority

✔ Want to feel valued, needed, and recognized for their positions

✔ Value how much money they earn

✔ Are dedicated to getting the work done, when they have clear job descriptions

✔ Believe they have the ability to "shine as stars"

Generation Xers

Generation Xers in the workplace

✔ See work as a contract

✔ Want structure and direction and, given that, are self-reliant, striving to complete any task assigned to them

✔ Are more motivated when they're given the freedom to do things their own way, in spite of the rules

Millennials

Millennials in the workplace

✔ Are highly confident multi-taskers who seek enjoyment in what they do

✔ Are very entrepreneurial and goal oriented

✔ Are creative and unafraid to take risks

✔ Are tenacious when performing a project, but at the same time need flexibility

✔ Seek a balance between their work and family lives, seeing work as a means to an end

The culturally diverse workplace

Today's global world has spawned a growing mixture of nationalities and religions in the workplace. With the global expansion and connectedness of organizations, the increased mobility available to people, and the influx of students from other countries pursuing education in the United States, it's no wonder that our workplaces are becoming more culturally diverse.

So, what is culture? *Culture* is a shared system of values, beliefs, attitudes, expectations, and norms for behavior. People acquire culture as they grow into adulthood. The cultural system, embedded in people's brains, acts like a filter as they watch people from other cultures behave in ways different than they would. This cultural filter often leads people to stereotype other people, often in negative ways, and attribute intentions or motivations to them that they don't have.

In looking at the people you hire and employees at all levels of your organization, you have to be aware of the influence of your own cultural filters, as well as the cultural filters of others. Keep in mind that stereotyping is a dangerous possibility when looking at cultural differences, but even more dangerous is ignoring differences.

Describing all the potential cultural differences that could be represented in your organization is beyond the scope of this book. Each organization, depending on where it's located and what kind of product or service it's delivering, encounters its own set of cultural differences.

What I can do, however, is give you some examples of differences in values and behaviors between cultures.

Cultural differences exist between different groups of people within the United States, as well as between Americans and people from other countries. You may notice distinct cultural differences as a Northerner in the South, for example, and vice versa.

Conception of self

The American conception of self is far more individualistic than the conception of self in some other countries, such as those in Asia.

Americans place a high value on independence. They are immodest and don't hesitate to promote themselves. They place a high value on individual freedom from any externally imposed constraints. Their myths, stories, and even the history of their country promote individualism.

Asian countries, for example, place a high value on cooperation and collaboration, on interdependence. They're more likely to be concerned with how their actions affect their entire group instead of how they affect them personally.

Reputation

Reputation is less important to Americans than it is for Asians.

For Americans, getting the job done is more important than reputation. In the fast pace of American business, reputations come and go. If people get the job done, their reputation doesn't matter.

Reputation is very important to Asians, however. Any action that will ruin someone's reputation is avoided. When someone in Japan or China does something that brings him or her shame, that person is willing to do whatever it takes to heal the shame, including sacrificing a job.

Gestures

Most people assume that the gestures they use are universal, but they aren't. Here are two significant differences among cultures:

✔ For Americans, gesturing to someone with your index finger means "come here." But Chinese people see gesturing to someone with your index finger as insulting.

✔ Americans shake hands when greeting people. Chinese people bow when greeting people.

✔ For Americans, giving a thumbs-up means everything is okay. People in Islamic countries see that as a rude sexual sign.

Time

The American concept of time is tighter and more precise than the concept of time in other countries, particularly Asian countries.

When Americans are supposed to attend a meeting scheduled for a particular time, they expect everyone to show up on time. Similarly when Americans set a deadline for a project to be completed, they expect that the project will be completed on time. Additionally, Americans are not particularly interested in the past, but they're very interested in the near future.

Asians view time more loosely. Nobody expresses concern if a meeting doesn't start exactly on time. Similarly, Asians don't worry if a deadline is missed. In other words, time for Asians is not so much an absolute as it is a suggestion. Additionally, Asians pay relatively more attention to the past and to the long-term future.

Interpersonal space

Interpersonal space (the space between two people that is comfortable for each) is very different for Americans and Chinese.

Americans are comfortable when they're 2 or 3 feet away from the person to whom they're talking. When people step closer to each other (unless, of course, it's an intimate relationship), they begin to feel uncomfortable.

Interpersonal space is much smaller for Chinese and Taiwanese people (probably because they grew up in far more crowded conditions than Americans). Even when there is ample space, Asians will end up standing closer to one another.

Social structure

Americans have a very informal, egalitarian view about social relationships, while Taiwanese people are far more formal and hierarchical.

In the United States, although people are most comfortable with their social equals, social status is minimized. It isn't unusual to see people from different social levels comfortably interact with one another at a business meeting or a social gathering.

Taiwanese people "know their position" and have specific customs and rules for behavior when meeting with people at different levels in the hierarchy.

Business relationships

Americans are more task oriented, while many Asians are more relationship oriented.

"Complete the task first, and then socialize" is the mantra for Americans. Socializing is far less important than getting the job done. American business associates tend to be more aloof.

Taiwanese people see the maintenance of a harmonious relationship as a higher priority than getting tasks done. When doing business, they socialize so business associates get to know each other. Allocating the correct social time is seen as necessary by Taiwanese people, even if it delays a contract.

Confrontation and conflict

Americans have no problem with confrontation. For Chinese people, direct confrontation is unacceptable.

Americans are willing to directly confront and/or criticize people. They have no problem discussing controversial topics and offering personal opinions. Their focus is on the issue, not on what other people are thinking about them when they offer their opinions.

Chinese avoid direct confrontation. In fact, direct confrontation or conflict over issues in a discussion is frowned upon. Chinese avoid open criticism, and controversial topics. Their focus is on maintaining harmony.

The technologically sophisticated workplace

The explosion of information technology had its small beginning several decades ago with the creation of the Internet. It slowly grew, spawning varieties of computers and spreading information and communication to millions of users. In the last 15 years, the World Wide Web has mushroomed into a plethora of technologically sophisticated communication devices, devices that are significantly changing the way business is being done around the world.

This new information/communication technology calls for new competencies that you have to consider when you're in the process of identifying successors for key positions during the development, implementation, and maintenance of your succession plan.

In the following sections, I cover the three primary categories of information technology.

Cloud computing

In the past, people stored everything on their personal computers. In today's world, people are storing more and more — from photos and videos to e-mail to financial records — online. Instead of storing the data on your computer, you're storing it "in the cloud."

Storing data online not only can be safer (for example, it protects the data if your computer crashes) but also makes the data accessible from any other Internet-connected device anywhere in the world.

Not only does the cloud give you access to your data from anywhere, it also consistently provides you with the latest versions of web applications.

Mobile computing and phone apps

Cellphones as communication devices are becoming a thing of the past. They're rapidly morphing into mobile computing devices. The embrace of smartphones has spawned the development of countless software applications (apps) designed specifically for them.

Mobile computing to access the Internet is becoming the norm. Cellphones are increasingly allowing users to do what they used to do on their desktop computers and laptops. The use of smartphones has increased dramatically, both for personal and business use. Some experts predict that sales of mobile devices will outnumber sales of personal computers within a few years.

Almost every employee in your workplace probably has a cellphone, which they bring to work and use throughout the day for everything from personal matters to searching for and finding information helpful to their jobs.

Social media

Social media is today's ultimate form of communicating and collaborating. It takes many forms:

✔ **Collaborative websites:** These websites allow people to collaborate from different physical locations via the Internet. They include Dabbleboard (www.dabbleboard.com), ProjectPier (www.projectpier.org), Project2Manage (www.project2manage.com), Smartsheet (www.smartsheet.com), and Spicebird (www.spicebird.com), to name just a few.

✔ **Blogs and microblogs:** These sites are maintained by individuals who regularly publish posts, which can contain everything from text to photos to videos, on any subject. Some blogs function as a kind of personal online diary, others as a discourse on a particular topic, and others as advertising of a particular individual or company. Microblogs typically have shorter posts than blogs do.

✔ **Social-networking sites:** A social-networking site allows users to connect with friends in an online community. Many social-networking sites allow people to find people with similar interests. Facebook (www.facebook.com), Twitter (www.twitter.com), LinkedIn (www.linkedin.com), and Google Plus (http://plus.google.com) are some of the main social-networking sites.

✔ **Virtual-content communities:** Virtual-content communities are sites where you share particular types of content. Two examples are YouTube (www.youtube.com), which is the world's biggest video-sharing site, and Flickr (www.flickr.com), a major photo-sharing site.

✔ **Social bookmarking:** This type of social media enables users to save and share web pages that they find interesting. Examples are Google Reader (http://reader.google.com), Delicious (www.delicious.com), and CiteULike (www.citeulike.org).

✔ **Internal social media networks:** Employees can securely share ideas, news, and other information in real time with each other on sites such as Chatter (www.chatter.com) and Yammer (www.yammer.com). These media networks are accessible only to employees of the subscribing organization.

The Impact of the Key Trends

Before you can make adjustments to your succession plan to help you adapt to these trends in today's workplace, you need to know a little bit about their impact on the workplace.

The multigenerational workplace

As the workplace becomes more multigenerational, differences between generations can be helpful — but they also can cause problems for an organization.

Here are some of the benefits of a multigenerational workplace:

- ✔ Newer generations bring new skills to the workplace, particularly technological and communication skills that can help improve productivity and performance in any department.

- ✔ Older generations bring order and discipline to the workplace that can, if done constructively, be helpful to younger generations.

- ✔ Younger generations' passion for learning can spur the organization to offer new training programs that could benefit every generation in the organization.

- ✔ The need to be creative and innovative among younger generations can be very helpful in multigenerational problem-solving meetings.

However, a multigenerational workplace also brings with it some challenges:

- ✔ Tensions can occur among people of different generations due to misunderstandings or differences in beliefs about basic concepts, such as time and responsibility.

- ✔ Different work and life balance expectations among generations can cause conflict.

- ✔ Widely different styles of communication between generations can cause tension due to the differing generational experiences with communication technologies. For example, Veterans grew up in a world without computers, while Millennials grew up in a world of technological fluency.

The culturally diverse workplace

As the market becomes more global and applicants for key positions become more culturally diverse, having a diverse workforce can have both a positive and a negative impact on your organization.

Here are some of the benefits of a culturally diverse workplace:

- ✔ A culturally diverse workforce gives you a better ability to understand the diverse international market.

✔ Given today's more culturally diverse customer base, having a culturally diverse organization can help you interact more effectively with your customers and achieve greater customer satisfaction.

✔ Greater cultural diversity in your organization brings with it a range of personal experiences that offer you different perspectives when it comes to decision making and problem solving, as well as to the application of different operational skills and strategies.

✔ In today's competitive marketplace, organizations need to be flexible and creative to keep up with the competition. A culturally diverse workplace can bring you more flexibility and creativity.

✔ The more prepared your organization is for changes in cultural demographics, the better prepared you'll be for changes in cultural diversity in the market and in the pool of applicants available for your key positions.

✔ Diverse cultural viewpoints, knowledge, and experience can help you develop and implement new approaches that can increase productivity and profits.

However, a culturally diverse workplace also brings with it some challenges:

✔ Cultural diversity can lead people to become ethnocentric, believing in the superiority of their own ethnic group.

✔ Cultural diversity often brings with it stereotyping, which is the pigeonholing of people by their culture and unfairly attributing characteristics to them that they may not have.

✔ Becoming ethnocentric and stereotyping can be disadvantageous to minorities in the workplace, especially if there is a cultural imbalance in the power structure of the organization.

✔ A culturally diverse team may have trouble coming to agreement about courses of action.

✔ In some organizations, cultural diversity can lead to *reverse discrimination* (discrimination felt by one or more people in the ethnic majority who feel they've been unfairly discriminated against because of the minority).

✔ Cultural diversity can lead to miscommunications because of language difficulties or the differences between meanings of words and concepts in different cultures.

✔ Cultural diversity can interfere with the achievement of project goals in a timely manner, because of differences among cultures and concepts of time.

The technologically sophisticated workplace

There is absolutely no doubt that information technology and social media are radically changing the way work is done. Overall, the effects of newer technology are a positive influence on your organization, but technology also can create problems.

Here are just some of the benefits of a technologically sophisticated workplace:

- ✔ Your organization can use social-networking tools to improve communication and productivity among employees.

- ✔ Social media provides your organization with tools to easily market its products and/or services.

- ✔ Your organization can use social media to help develop strong relationships with its customer base.

- ✔ Social media can help build a sense of organization-wide interdependence by keeping employees more connected.

- ✔ Social media is a tool for gathering a tremendous amount of data about your customers, as well as getting their feedback.

However, a technologically sophisticated workplace also brings with it some challenges:

- ✔ If it isn't regulated by specific guidelines, employees' use of the Internet and social media can lead to a significant waste of time, reducing productivity.

- ✔ If the right precautions and policies aren't implemented in your organization, some employees will use social media to engage in negative activities, such as cyber-bullying.

- ✔ Social media can be used to reveal confidential information — such as information about fellow employees, trade secrets, or client secrets — which can be a very serious problem for any organization.

- ✔ Some employees may use social-networking sites or their blogs to post unflattering or outright offensive opinions about their employers or co-workers. Other employees may use the Internet to publish defamatory, false material about your organization or a competitor. Still other employees may use the Internet and social media at work to download copyrighted movies, music, and pornographic material.

Modifying Your Succession Plan to Adjust to the Key Trends

The good news is this: You have the ability to make more accurate decisions about processes, procedures, and people during the course of your succession planning armed with the information in this chapter.

Here are some suggestions for incorporating what you know about the three key trends into your succession-planning process:

- ✔ **When forming your succession-planning team, include a mixture of generations.** During team discussions, while developing your succession plan, make sure that the different generational viewpoints are heard, weighed, and considered in developing descriptions of competencies needed for key positions.

- ✔ **If cultural diversity is evident in your organization, reflect that diversity in your planning team.** Make sure that the different cultural viewpoints are heard, weighed, and considered during the development of your succession plan.

- ✔ **Identify the person in your organization who is most up-to-date and knowledgeable about information technology and social media.** Include that person as a member of your planning team, or at least seek input from him or her periodically, as needed.

- ✔ **When determining competencies for key positions, make sure that they're up to date with respect to advances in information technology and social media.**

- ✔ **When you construct job descriptions for both evaluation purposes and recruiting, make sure they're up to date with advances in information technology and social media.**

- ✔ **When determining competencies for key positions, make sure that they reflect an awareness of and some sensitivity to multigenerational and cultural differences.**

- ✔ **When implementing your succession plan, use social media to get timely feedback on its effectiveness from everyone involved in the process, as well as any candidates being interviewed.**

- ✔ **Throughout the course of your succession planning and implementation, use social media as a platform for team members to periodically communicate progress on their assigned portion of the plan.** If your company is spread over geographical areas or is global, use a collaborative site such as WebEx (www.webex.com) for periodic, virtual succession-planning meetings.

✔ **Use a variety of social media for recruiting candidates.** See Chapter 14 for more information.

✔ **When developing internal personnel for transfers or promotions to key positions, make sure that their coaching, mentoring, and/or training include multigenerational and cultural awareness sessions.**

These strategies will help you be more prepared for market changes and remain competitive as you develop and implement your succession plan.

The more people in your organization are aware of the three trends, the easier it will be for you to develop and implement your succession plan. Create organizational awareness by:

✔ **Conducting awareness training sessions for all employees that explores both generational and cultural differences:** The training should include guidelines and/or checklists for participants to help them explore differences. It also should include exercises in listening and communicating to help participants become more sensitive to generational and cultural differences.

✔ **Conducting social media training for all employees that emphasizes both the use of social media and parameters for using it:** The training should emphasize the constructive use of social media as a tool to help your organization be more productive and build communication among your employees as well as with your customers. It also should include a presentation of communication etiquette when using social media. The training should include some do's and don'ts expressed through social-media policy that you construct for your organization. It also should include exercises in listening and communicating to help participants become more sensitive to generational and cultural differences.

The more people in your organization are aware of the three current trends in today's workplace and their impact on your organization, the easier it will be for you to develop, implement, and maintain your succession plan and respond to these trends.

Part V
The Part of Tens

"Okay, we all know how this is done. There are 4 of you and only 3 regional manager openings. Margaret—start the music."

In this part . . .

This wouldn't be a *For Dummies* book without a Part of Tens. In this part, you find ten common mistakes to avoid and ten ways to keep your plan alive and thriving. If you want to make the most of the limited time you have, this little part is for you.

Chapter 14

Ten Mistakes That Sabotage Succession Plans

In This Chapter

▶ Uncovering costly mistakes

▶ Steering clear of pitfalls

*N*o succession plan ever gets developed and implemented perfectly. Despite your best intentions, you'll probably end up making a few mistakes along the way. Some will be minor. Others could seriously impact the success of your plan.

In this chapter, you find ten of the most common mistakes that can sabotage a succession plan, along with tips and suggestions for helping you avoid these mistakes. Pay careful attention to these tips and suggestions. They'll help you create and implement a successful succession plan.

Not Making Succession Planning a Priority

With all the other things going on in your organization, it's easy to put succession planning on the back burner. Don't let this happen.

Here are some suggestions for preventing this kind of mistake:

✔ **Make your succession plan an important component of your strategic plan.** This will force you to pay attention to it every time you have reason to refer to or revise your strategic plan.

✔ **In weekly manager meetings, list succession planning as a priority item on your agenda.** Every week, managers will review issues, progress, and developments related to your succession plan.

✔ **Involve one of your top managers as the leader of your succession-planning team.** Not only will this signal top management support for succession planning, but it will also communicate the importance of succession planning to other people in the organization.

✔ **Set up milestones for every aspect of your succession plan.** Select a team member to be accountable for reaching each of those milestones. If a milestone is missed, take immediate action to correct the situation.

✔ **Send everyone involved a weekly e-mail that reviews the status of the succession-planning process.** This includes all team members, top management, the department manager affected by the change, and anyone in the organization who is assigned to carry out a particular step in the process.

Don't put your succession plan on the back burner. Keep it going and always in the foreground with other key organizational priorities.

Not Developing a Full Plan

Some organizations don't get into enough detail when developing their succession plan.

Any succession plan must include detailed steps and processes for several core components:

✔ **Clear, measurable statements of objectives:** You need clear, measurable objectives in order to set up your desired outcomes, along with timelines and accountability in any action plans associated with your succession plan.

✔ **Competencies:** Make sure that the set of competencies for each position in your succession plan is up to date and stated in detail. All too often, succession planners don't pay enough attention to competency details.

✔ **Talent pools:** Sometimes, succession planners, eager to fill a needed position, don't pay enough attention to possible sources for successor candidates. The implementation of your succession plan will go much more smoothly if you've taken the time to conduct a detailed exploration of possible candidate sources.

✔ **Action plans:** Some succession planners develop a reasonably detailed plan but fall short in establishing action plans designed to make sure that the plan is completely followed. You need to establish a well-defined action plan for every aspect of your succession plan. Action plans should include timelines, milestones, and the people accountable for making sure that whatever is supposed to happen happens.

✔ **A link to your strategic plan:** Because they're totally focused on filling critical positions, some planners fail to expand their thinking to the strategic-planning level. A good succession plan doesn't just focus on immediate or pending needs to fill key positions. It also focuses on the future. The best way to do that is to link your succession plan to your overall strategic plan so you can anticipate the kinds of competencies needed for positions in the future.

Not Aligning Your Plan to the Marketplace

The marketplace is constantly changing. New products suddenly appear. New services are offered. New competitors suddenly pop up. Any one of these changes in the marketplace can significantly affect the kinds of competencies needed for key positions.

Here are a few tips to help you align your succession plan to the marketplace:

✔ **When forming your succession-planning team, designate one team member as the "marketplace expert."** As the plan is being developed, that team member is responsible for monitoring changes in the marketplace and offering suggestions and adjustments to any competency definitions as a result of those changes. That team member also should continue to monitor changes in the marketplace during the implementation of your succession plan, again offering suggestions and adjustments to any competency definitions as a result of those changes.

✔ **Pay attention to what colleagues have to say in professional association meetings about new products and/or services.** Consider the implications of what you hear for your succession plan.

✔ **Pay particular attention to speeches, press releases, and books generated by your competitors.** Make sure you're aware of any new and innovative changes taking place.

Not Considering the Changing Composition of the Workforce

Due to longer lifespans and economic conditions, today's workforce is composed of more generations than ever before. Each generation has its own set of values, expectations, and work habits. The need to deal with these differences among generations may call for new competencies, particularly in management and leadership positions.

The increased percentage of millennials in the workplace, bringing with them all their computer and social media expertise, is definitely affecting how things get done. New technologies call for new competencies — and you need to consider this issue in your succession plan.

In addition, the composition of the workforce is changing. Many organizations are experiencing a significant increase in cultural diversity among their employees. You need to be aware of this diversity and any implications for redefining job competencies.

Finally, with millions of Baby Boomers poised to retire in the relatively near future, be sure to acquire and categorize as much of their knowledge, competencies, and expertise as possible, and start planning today for the open positions that their departures will generate.

 Having a competent workforce is an important factor in your organizational success. Make sure you consider the changing composition of the workforce as you develop and implement your succession plan. (See Chapter 13 for more on today's changing workplace.)

Not Getting Support from the Top

Your succession plan won't succeed without top management support. More than any other individuals, the CEO and top managers are cognizant of the organizational mission and aware of what needs to be done to accomplish that mission.

The CEO, in particular, must be a strong supporter of the plan. Ideally, the CEO is the one who initiates succession planning in the first place, by forming a team to develop the plan.

 If your organization is a smaller organization, encourage the CEO to lead the succession-planning team. That, alone, signals his or her strong support.

If your organization is larger, make sure your succession planning team continually keeps the CEO informed about the team's progress through weekly reports or e-mails at the end of every team meeting. The CEO and other top managers also should sit in on succession-planning meetings from time to time.

Make top managers an active part of the succession-planning process. For example, when a particular candidate surfaces as a very probable successor, have top managers mentor the candidate.

Not Effectively Communicating Your Plan

Communication is one of the most important components of successful succession planning. Change makes many people anxious. The more they know about what's happening, the more comfortable they'll feel.

Here are some tips to help you effectively communicate your succession plan:

- ✔ If you have a board of directors, make sure they're informed of your succession-planning process, every step of the way. Ask the board to appoint a spokesperson to communicate the succession plan to shareholders and other relevant parties.

- ✔ Continually update your website with announcements about succession-planning events.

- ✔ If you have an employee and/or customer newsletter, include a special column in each issue that updates readers on the progress of succession planning.

- ✔ Post succession-planning updates on company bulletin boards and update them regularly to let everyone know what's happening with the succession-planning process.

- ✔ Circulate a very readable, clearly written version of your completed succession plan throughout your organization, and encourage managers to review and discuss it in staff meetings.

- ✔ If your organization is a smaller organization, have the CEO meet with all employees at least quarterly to bring them up to date about the succession-planning process.

Effectively communicating your plan will help to quell any negative rumors circulating in your organization. It also will stimulate some people to express their interest as potential successors to particular key positions, thereby enlarging your talent pool.

Not Getting Organizational Support

Even if your succession plan is focused primarily on the CEO and/or top management, it must have support throughout your entire organization. Changes taking place in key positions may stimulate uneasiness among employees — they may begin to worry about how their own jobs will be affected.

Here are some tips for quelling such uneasiness and getting organizational support:

- ✔ **Build overall support among employees by fully informing them of any changes about to take place.** Being upfront and honest will go a long way toward quelling any uneasiness.

- ✔ **Introduce your employees to new successors after they've been selected.** Give the employees opportunities to get to know and become comfortable with successors in key positions particularly relevant to their jobs.

- ✔ **Fully inform employees about succession-planning events taking place.** This tactic will help employees see themselves as members of a larger, supportive organizational team, rather than as people just doing jobs.

- ✔ **Encourage employees to provide their own ideas and suggestions for the succession-planning process.** The more opportunities that they have to provide their input, the more supportive they'll be of the plan and ultimately of the individuals who move into the open positions.

Keep employees in the succession-planning loop, and directly solicit their support. Gaining strong and widespread support for your succession-planning process will make its implementation proceed smoothly and with fewer problems.

Not Using Social Media Effectively

In implementing your succession plan, you want access to as large a pool of qualified applicants as you can find. In the past, organizations have accomplished this goal by placing ads in various newspapers and magazines, on recruitment websites such as Monster (www.monster.com), and sometimes even on TV.

This age of social media offers organizations an entirely new way to find qualified candidates. Through social-networking site such as Facebook (`www.facebook.com`), LinkedIn (`www.linkedin.com`), and Twitter (`www.twitter.com`), people are networking more than ever before. More than three of every four employees use social media to connect with other people. Facebook, LinkedIn, and Twitter combined have over 535 million users. What a large potential source of qualified candidates!

Facebook is the largest social networking site. Over 400 million users connect themselves with friends, family, business associates, and, more recently, organizations. You can use this Facebook network to find qualified candidates in several ways:

- ✔ **Create a Facebook Page, which identifies your business and all the exciting things happening with it.** Post job openings. Create a positive, enticing page that will attract people who are looking for a job. Make sure you continuously keep your Facebook Page up to date with exciting new information.

- ✔ **Post a job for free in the Facebook Marketplace (**`http://apps.facebook.com/marketplace`**).** Create an ad that is essentially a job description, including the competencies you're looking for.

- ✔ **Post a Facebook Ad (**`www.facebook.com/advertising`**).** A Facebook Ad will cost you some money, but it'll enable you to precisely target the kind of candidate audience that you're looking for.

LinkedIn is a little more specialized than Facebook. It's an interconnected network of over 65 million professionals representing 170 industries from 200 countries around the world. You can use this LinkedIn network to find qualified candidates in several ways:

- ✔ **Post available jobs.** Because LinkedIn is a professional network, it will narrow your search to professionals.

- ✔ **Build connections with colleagues, former employees, people you meet in professional associations, friends, and so on.** Somewhere there is someone who knows someone who knows someone who may be interested in your opening.

- ✔ **Use the Network Activity box to send a message out to the network that you're looking for a particular kind of candidate to fill a position.**

The more you network through social media, the more you increase the chances that you'll be able to find the kinds of candidates you need to fill open positions.

Not Effectively Monitoring Your Plan

You can't just develop a succession plan, implement it, and walk away. You need to continually monitor your plan to make sure that everything is working out the way it's supposed to.

Your succession plan includes measurable objectives. Behind each objective is a process designed to achieve it. Set up a schedule and designate succession-planning team members to be accountable for monitoring each process, as well as for assessing the effectiveness of the overall plan at least once a year.

Invariably, monitoring the implementation processes will uncover some things that you need to improve. (See Chapter 6 for a more detailed description of monitoring your succession plan.)

Not Providing Enough Support for the Successor

After you've hired a successor, the game isn't over. You need to give the successor the kind of support that helps him or her meld into the organization. Here are some things you can do to provide support to the successor:

- **Familiarize the successor with your organization well before the transition even takes place.** The more familiar the successor is with your organization, the more easily and more comfortably he or she will slide into the position.

- **Familiarize relevant employees about the successor.** Have the successor attend meetings and interact with employees, so they get to know the successor and feel comfortable with the change about to take place.

- **Provide the successor with as much information as you can about the ins and outs of the position.**

See Chapter 11 for more on paving the way to a smooth transition.

Chapter 15

Ten Ways to Keep Your Succession Plan Alive

In This Chapter
▶ Nurturing your succession plan
▶ Giving your plan an environment it can thrive in

*J*ust as a plant flourishes in the right soil, your succession plan will be significantly more successful if the right organizational climate nurtures it. Some organizations are so fractured and compartmentalized that getting the right coordination and support for any succession plan is nearly impossible. That's not the kind of organization you want. In this chapter, you find ten suggestions for creating the kind of organizational environment that will help you successfully create a succession plan and keep it alive.

As you read this chapter, don't be put off by the amount of time, effort, and resources some of the advice will require. When it comes to handling departures and planning for positions that don't even exist today, the future of your organization is at stake. You need to invest the resources to do what it takes to be prepared for any contingency.

Build a Competency Culture

Your succession plan must define the competencies required of successors or new hires. And this process of defining competencies will go more smoothly if your organization has a *competency culture*, an organizational culture in which everyone is

✔ Aware of the specific competencies needed to perform his or her job

✔ Motivated to develop his or her competencies to the highest level

To create a competency culture in your organization, start with the CEO and top managers; then move to other levels of management and supervisors; and finally, have managers meet with their employees. What do you discuss in these meetings? The competencies needed to perform their jobs. Ask everyone in your organization — from the CEO to the receptionist — what competencies are required to do that job.

Your HR department already may have this kind of information, but it helps to start with discussions with the people who are currently in those positions.

The purpose of these meetings is to focus everyone on competencies — and while you're at it, to encourage them to further develop those competencies. Offer educational and training activities to help people develop their skills.

Yes, these meetings will take time, effort, and resources. But in the long run, the information you gather and the message you communicate will make your succession-planning process much easier. You won't have to construct a set of competencies every time you have to fill a key position.

And there are side benefits, too: Managers and their employees will end up with a mutual set of expectations about how work should be performed. Employees will have a clearer understanding of what their managers expect of them. And all this emphasis on individual growth and development has a positive motivational impact.

Construct an All-Inclusive Succession Plan

Succession planners typically focus on particular positions, such as the CEO or some other key position deemed invaluable to the organization. Yes, some positions are more important to your organization than others. But don't lose sight of the fact that every employee makes an important contribution.

Broaden your thinking about succession planning. Building on your competency culture (see the preceding section), make your succession plan an all-inclusive one. The processes outlined in your plan should be applicable anywhere in the organization at any time. If you've developed such a plan, your organization won't skip a beat if someone leaves or if some change in the marketplace or overall strategic plan calls for new sets of competencies.

Think of the composite collection of your succession-planning processes as a large control center machine with many switches. A top manager suddenly departs, and you flip the right switch to activate a process; a key artist retires from the marketing department, and you flip another switch; and so on.

The hard work in creating an all-inclusive succession plan is upfront. After you've completed it and implemented it, the work becomes routine. It's there for you to tap into whenever you need to do so.

Involve Managers in the Planning Process and Get Their Support

In many ways, your managers are the backbone of your organization. They're connected to every aspect of your organization's functions. More than anyone else, they're in touch with the kinds of day-to-day competencies needed by their employees for getting work done.

If your organization is small, consider having all your managers be part of the succession-planning team. If your organization is larger, keep managers informed and involved along the way. Here's how:

- ✔ After your planning team has outlined the ingredients of your succession plan, present it to managers to get their feedback and input.

- ✔ Thereafter, keep every manager abreast of the progress you're making, and solicit their feedback and suggestions.

- ✔ When the planning team is developing processes for dealing with specific key positions relevant to specific managers (such as an important IT specialist), invite that manager to a planning meeting to get his or her input.

Ask managers to submit a set of competencies to the succession-planning team that includes their own competencies, as well as the competencies of every employee who reports to them.

The more managers are involved in your succession planning, the more they'll feel ownership of it, and the more likely they'll be to support it.

Link Your Succession Plan Directly to Your Strategic Plan

The selection of a successor must be guided by the organization's core strategy, which is articulated in its overall strategic plan — its values, its vision, and its mission. Your strategic plan tells everyone where your organization has been, where it is now, and where you want it to go. So, it's essential that your succession plan be closely linked to your strategic plan.

This linkage will help your succession-planning team in several ways:

- ✔ When you build your database of potentially needed competencies, your strategic plan will tell you what competencies you need to emphasize.

- ✔ The portion of your strategic plan that deals with projected changes will provide succession planners with a framework and guidelines for any new competencies that may be needed.

- ✔ Your strategic plan will constantly change over time, due to changes in the marketplace and/or changes in the direction your organization is choosing to go. Linked to your strategic plan, your succession plan will have the up-to-date information you need to adjust to such changes.

- ✔ Linking your succession plan to your strategic plan will keep you continually focused on the organizational mission in the successor selection process.

Link Your Succession Plan to Your Mission Statement

All too often, mission statements are cleverly crafted, framed, and hung on walls, but most people don't really know their organizational mission. Use the development of your succession plan as an opportunity to align employees throughout your organization with your organizational mission.

When you present the plan to employees in meetings, begin by highlighting the importance of your succession plan in ensuring that the organizational mission will continue to be fulfilled, even if a key position suddenly changes.

Assuming you've developed a competency culture (covered earlier in this chapter), encourage employees to tie what they do to the organizational mission. Ask the employees to establish and commit to a personal developmental plan that will enhance their competencies and contribute to the organization's quest to fulfill its mission.

The purpose of these activities is not only to improve the quality of your workforce, but also to generate the support of your employees for your succession plan.

Turn Your Succession Plan into an Ongoing Process

Don't make your succession plan a one-time event. Don't allow yourself to be put in a place where a sudden departure or important shift in the marketplace catches you by surprise and forces you to scramble to put some steps together as quickly as possible.

Numerous benefits accrue when your succession planning is an ongoing process:

- ✔ Succession planning will function more proactively and will be better able to monitor and assess the organization's workforce needs.
- ✔ When it's linked to your strategic plan, succession planning will be better able to proactively address both current and projected competencies.
- ✔ Your succession plan will be ready at a moment's notice when you experience unexpected departures.
- ✔ Succession planning will facilitate smoother transitions when successors are selected to fill open positions.

 An ongoing succession-planning process is as important to the success of your organization as your ongoing strategic plan is.

Plan to Change

Succession plans shouldn't be written in stone. They need to be flexible enough to adapt to all kinds of unexpected events. For example:

- ✔ Your CEO planned to retire in six months, but he suddenly dies of a heart attack. You've done some searching for successors, but your time frame has completely changed.

- ✔ Your best salesperson is offered and accepts an attractive job in another organization. Suddenly, you're faced with losing a significant number of sales.

- ✔ During the implementation of your plan, you discover that the procedures you designed to build an easily accessible talent pool aren't working anywhere near as well as you wanted them to work.

These are just a few examples of things that can happen that will require you to adjust your plan. The more flexible your succession plan, the more likely it will be successful.

Emphasize the Development of Internal Candidates

Look first at home. The more often you can develop someone in your organization to move to a key position that has just become available or may be open down the road, the more employees throughout your organization will be motivated to further develop their own competencies.

Here are some ways you can focus on developing the talented people you already have:

- ✔ Offer training opportunities to employees, especially those in key positions.

- ✔ Send employees with the potential to become successors to special workshop sessions or professional association meetings to help them develop their competencies.

- ✔ Assign coaches to employees who are seen as potential candidates to assume key positions.

- ✔ If you select a successor from within your organization who appears to have all the competencies needed, assign him or her a mentor to ensure a smooth transition.

Succession planning doesn't always involve someone being promoted to a higher position. Employees often make lateral moves to position that they enjoy more or are better suited for.

What happens when you emphasize the development of internal candidates? You get improved employee motivation, morale, and satisfaction.

Build and Maintain an External Network of Successor Candidates

You can build and maintain a network of successor candidates outside your organization by accumulating a database comprised of the following:

- ✔ People you meet in professional association meetings
- ✔ People you meet in training sessions
- ✔ Referrals from friends and colleagues
- ✔ Executive search firms
- ✔ Employment agencies
- ✔ Competitors
- ✔ Connections you make through the use of social media, such as Facebook, Twitter, and LinkedIn

Developing people internally has its own merits (see the preceding section), but finding candidates from external sources gives you the opportunity to integrate new ways of looking at how the business should be run.

Continually Monitor and Adjust Your Plan Where Needed

Monitoring the implementation and overall effectiveness of your succession plan is key. You need to know where it's working well and where it isn't.

Here are some suggestions for making sure that your plan is properly monitored:

- ✔ When you finish your succession plan, establish action plans for each specific goal or activity in your plan. The action plans should include the following:

- A clear statement of each goal or activity. Make sure you state it in a way that's measurable (for example, with a specific deadline).

- Detailed, specific steps for achieving each goal.

- Milestones and timelines for accomplishing each goal.

- Which team members are accountable for achieving each goal.

✔ Appoint one succession-planning team member as the person with the overall responsibility of making sure that those action plans are followed.

✔ Establish periodic meetings of the succession-planning team to review the effectiveness of the plan at every step and to make sure that specific actions are being carried out to keep the plan aligned with its objectives and the organization's mission.

If you don't monitor your succession plan and assess its effectiveness, you'll have no way of knowing how well it's working or what you could do to make it work even better.

Index

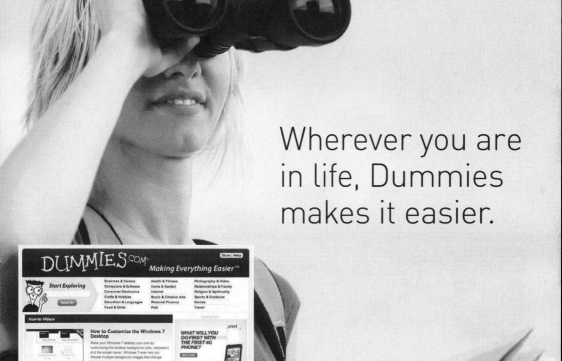

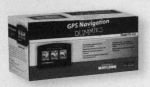

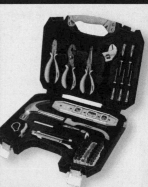